To Jo Ann
Best Wishes

Slorie Solomon Apple

THEY WERE STRANGERS

THEY WERE STRANGERS

A Family History

Slovie Solomon Apple

VANTAGE PRESS
New York

Published by Vantage Press, Inc.
516 West 34th Street, New York, New York 10001

Manufactured in the United States of America
ISBN: 0-533-11057-2

Library of Congress Catalog Card No.: 94-90070

0 9 8 7 6 5 4 3 2 1

I wish to acknowledge the valuable help I received from the distinguished books listed in the bibliography.

—Slovie Solomon Apple

Contents

THEY WERE
STRANGERS

Prologue

The pages that follow contain the story of the heroic generations of one family who were cruelly uprooted from their homelands by anti-Semitism. They were dispersed and scattered to make new homes, new lives, in other lands, with only their faith and courage.

However, in the new lands it wasn't long before anti-Semitism would rear its ugly head again. With love and fear people would send their children off to new countries to survive, always with hopes of finding safer havens, new beginnings, lives of freedom.

They were strangers in these new lands and suffered much hardship, but they always conducted themselves honorably, worked hard, and had a deep love for family and a strong belief in their religion.

This book is dedicated to the memory of my beloved mother, Clara Rothman, and my grandparents. It is written for our family, my children, and grandchildren.

My thanks to Samuel Apple, my husband, for his love and support.

My thanks and appreciation to Claudia Crawford, Humanities Department, College of Liberal Arts, University of Minnesota, whose encouragement and understanding made this book a reality.

Part I

Benjamin's Journey

Chapter 1

The Starting Point

Of the many anti-Semitic uprisings at a time that dispersed our Jews around the world, I have no knowledge of which one brought our great-grandparents Mordecai and Raizel Rothman to Soroki, Russia.

In the atlas Soroki is a tiny dot on the map of Russia. It is about two hundred miles from Kiev. It sits precisely 48.09 north latitude and 28.17 east longitude, bordered on one side by the Russian Ukraine and on the other by Moldavia.

It doesn't look very important, but it is. It's a starting point, a point where the first roots of our family began, and this brings a feeling of overwhelming significance. We have a history!

Soroki is located near the Dneister River, an area that Russian troops passed as they crossed Moldavia returning from frequent wars or pogroms (massacres).

The Rothman family, Mordecai, Raizel, and their son, Benjamin, lived in Czarist Russia under Alexander II. It was a Russia that had been through unrest and disorder, especially in the agricultural districts.

The wealthy nobles and favorites of the court owned the land. They also owned the serfs (peasants), who were slaves in bondage to their masters.

These serfs worked the land and were given very little to live on. They owed their lives and families to the landlords. After many, many years they began to rebel. What they wanted were reforms and social justices.

Russia was trying to become an industrial country, but industrial growth was slow. Because of this, factory workers, too, began to show unrest, with protests and demands for more benefits. They were becoming troublesome to the government, to which was added a brutal police force to snuff out subversion and revolution. Trusted military men, who could carry out barbaric atrocities, were put in high government offices. One of these, an officer named Prokhov, was in charge of the area around Soroki.

Restrictions were many. Very few Russians could travel outside the country. Spying was widespread. The secret police would infiltrate into communities and groups and inform the authorities of those who violated the laws. Punishment usually was exile to Siberia or death by torture.

Czar Alexander II, trying to prevent revolution, made the decision to abolish serfdom. Serfs were granted their personal liberty but were not allowed to leave the land.

Alexander came up with a plan to hand the lands over to the serfs gradually. The serfs would be able to purchase the land, making payments for it for a number of years, but each serf would not own the land individually. The title would be held by the village commune, who would manage the land and collect taxes on it.

In 1861 the serfs were freed from bondage to their masters. This meant the peasants could no longer be bought or sold or cruelly punished by floggings. They could now leave, but only with a passport, which was difficult to obtain.

Those who stayed found the land badly managed by the villages. Crop yields were low, and payment on the land could not be met.

People became angry when food shortages occurred. Revolutionaries wanted the serfs to have the land free of charge. Serfs felt cheated and many rioted, burned properties, and murdered. These situations between the government and serfs were the cause for many pogroms carried out on the Jews.

Any time the government found itself at odds with a group, any group, the hysteria turned on the Jews. They were blamed for all things that went wrong with the government.

Terrorist organizations began forming. These were against the authoritative form of government; they wanted control to establish their own system. There were many attempts on Alexander's life. These unhappy circumstances set up the Jews as scapegoats of pogroms in towns, villages, and numerous communities.

These pogroms were demonstrations and riots leveled against Russian Jews. Thousands were brutally murdered. Hundreds more were taken prisoner and sent to labor camps, where they were subjected to the cruelest, most inhuman treatment. The object was to rid Russia of the Jews.

There was a long-term military conscription for Jewish boys. They were taken between the ages of twelve and eighteen. The term of their military service was twenty-five years.

There were long hours of forced hard labor in the freezing clime of Siberia. They were inadequately clothed, and their food rations were often inedible. These were often purposely oversalted to give the men a killing thirst; then they were denied water to quench it.

6

This, together with illness and disease, was the death knell for many. Russia was a giant Jewish graveyard.

They went in as young men, and the few who survived came out feeble, broken, old men.

Many were converted under pressure of torture. Thousands of parents never saw their sons again.

It was this dreaded conscription and the deplorable conditions of everyday life without freedom that Mordecai would try to help his son to escape.

Chapter 2
In the Village of Soroki

About the middle of the nineteenth century there were about 5 million Jews in Russia. They were forced to live in a small area known as the Pale of Settlement. They were concentrated in an area close to three hundred thousand square miles, which was only about 4 percent of the Russian Empire.

Mordecai Rothman lived here near Soroki. He was engaged in what the government called retail commerce. More than half the inhabitants of the Pale had undertaken some form of this business. The government never talked about their difficulty in forging some kind of living. They were a miserably impoverished people.

"Businesses" were small, dilapidated stands along a roadside, selling almost anything, small shops, and those who sold goods door to door.

Mordecai had a small tailor shop where he repaired clothes and furs. This morning he stood, lost in thought, near his cutting table, his yarmulke perched atop his graying brown hair. Gently he stroked his goatee.

Now Mordecai was a law-abiding person though not a citizen, for Jews were not allowed to become citizens and were denied passports and papers of certification of birth issued to citizens.

Wearing his yarmulke was a silent act of defiance against the government's religious restrictions. Mordecai was a religious man. The unjust laws leveled against him because he was a Jew both angered and saddened him.

He got up on the table and sat cross-legged, sewing. Here he had command of a view from any point of the three intersecting streets in front of the shop. When he saw soldiers approaching, he quickly removed the yarmulke and put it in his vest next to his heart. Every once in a while he would put his hand over it and smile. It gave him great satisfaction, this cat-and-mouse game he played with the soldiers and his yarmulke.

Today concern and worry were showing on his face. It was a face a little too old for its thirty-eight years. It couldn't deny the strain of everyday living in the ghetto with its hard work, crowded conditions, and food shortages. Then there was the constant harassment by the government, the constant pressure to convert the Jews, and the worry over high taxes imposed on the small community that devastated them all.

Many in the crowded area became ill and died. They were buried at night, and there were no markers on the graves because of cemetery desecrations by rebelling peasants or soldiers.

Prokhov, the military man in charge of the Soroki area, was responsible for much of the terror and violence perpetrated against the Jews here. He did his job well. Testimony to that was his long stay in Soroki in the honored position he held in the government for taking care of the "Jewish problem" with his "solutions."

"Jews have nerve," he said. The nerve he spoke of was their raw courage. They were a proud people. They weakened physically, but their spirits were sustained by their religion.

Prokhov's solutions were to crowd the Jews into a small area among illiterate peasants and forbid their children any study, especially religious study. Every possible obstacle was put before the Jews to rob them of their livelihood and their dignity as men and women.

All day Mordecai's son, Benjamin, had been in his father's thoughts. Nearly fifteen, the boy was tall for his age and thin, with wiry brown hair and the darkest brown eyes. Soft-spoken and good, the boy was the light of Mordecai's life.

A little over a year ago he had become a bar mitzvah, which was forbidden. Mordecai could not have Benjamin grow up without a bar mitzvah, and besides, the boy wanted it. In Judaism he now would be considered a man, ready to take on the responsibilities of his religion.

The boy had been a dedicated scholar, often studying far into the night. He had made his parents proud as he read and chanted his *mafter* for the few friends gathered for the celebration, which was held in secret.

Mordecai and a man known as Reb Lazer taught Benjamin his Hebrew even though it was not permitted. Disobedience, if one was caught, was punishable by banishment to Siberia or instant death, since Russia was intent on doing away with Jews and their religion.

There had been a confiscation of Jewish prayer books, which were burned, but secretly some had been saved and were well hidden.

Mordecai was worried that his son could be called up for the military any day now. The sleepless nights were too many for him

9

to count. He couldn't tell anyone about his nightmares of Benjamin being taken away by army guards.

At home, Benjamin helped a few villagers work the small, weed-infested plots of land behind their homes, both owned by the government, since Jews were not allowed to own anything. They just paid the highest taxes.

Benjamin was readying the little plot for the spring planting. He would care for a few vegetables and, what he loved most, the two cherry trees at the edge of the field. He worked hard and long in the spring and through the long warm summer days and all through the fall. He didn't complain, because he enjoyed the satisfaction that came with planting, nurturing, and then watching the crops break through the earth to fruition. He liked doing all of it, but it was the delicate cherry blossoms, and later the abundant supply of sweet red cherries, that made him happiest.

Benjamin's parents would help him gather the share that went to the landowner and the very little that was allowed each family. Out of their meager portion Benjamin was taught to give part of it to another family, for being able to share made one happy and was a mitzvah.

The Russian winter had been harsh and long. There was very little work in the shop for Mordecai, but now with spring here he could do tailoring, sewing and repairing clothes. He often took work home and sewed by the light of a lamp or a candle.

At the end of the week, he worried if there was enough to pay rent, set some aside for taxes, and have a little left for the family. From that small amount Mordecai had been faithfully setting some aside for Benjamin to leave someday soon.

Whatever problems the family had, Mordecai, the head of the house, dealt with them. "Trouble was," he said, "as I grew older, the problems got bigger!"

Mordecai had always believed that with God's help there was a way to work things out. Today he came home with the weight of his problems on his shoulders. Time, among other things, was the enemy. His problems were time and money so Benjamin could leave.

Then, of course, there was the man Prokhov. These Jews were a dilemma to him, but the unpredictable Prokhov was just as much a problem to the Jews. One never knew if the quota for conscription would be posted, or if soldiers would come in the night and take the young men. It was Russian roulette Prokhov played with their lives, and they feared him with good reason.

Mordecai wondered, *Will there be time for Benjamin to leave?* He prayed there would be. Then unsettling rumors about the conscription began circulating, and Mordecai knew the heartbreaking decision had to be made now!

Plans had to be made immediately to smuggle Benjamin out. Mordecai's thoughts reverted back and forth from Benjamin to his wife, Raizel. He knew he had to impart the news of Benjamin leaving very soon—that night. The question was, How?

On his way home Mordecai, troubled, carried on conversations with himself. "Is this the only way to let the boy leave?" he muttered. Then he'd answer himself, "I know this is the only way." He'd shake his head. "The only way!"

He questioned God, "Why? I have only one child. Why should he have to leave?" Then he said a prayer and accepted what had to be. God's will had to be done.

Mordecai pondered over the right words to say to Raizel, but no matter how hard he tried, he knew this couldn't be done without inflicting great pain on this devoted, loving mother.

Reaching his home, he straightened his sagging shoulders, took a deep breath, then opened the door.

"Is that you, Mordecai? I'm so glad you're home."

He heard the welcoming warmth in his Raizel's voice. Then, closing the door on the hate and turmoil of the world outside, he went to greet her.

Chapter 3

Benjamin Departs

The first two days of the following week Benjamin spent saying his good-byes to just a few good friends. It was done quietly so as not to arouse any suspicion.

Raizel kept herself busy getting the boy's things ready. Gently she ripped the underarm lining of a jacket sleeve and sewed a small cloth pouch there, anchoring it with heavy thread. It would contain a few gold coins Mordecai had gotten and saved.

Benjamin came over and sat beside her, watching as she stitched away. She set the sewing aside and lovingly brushed his hair back from his face. Then her eyes hungrily scanned his face over and over as if to forge the memory of that moment. He was the golden season of her life.

This parting wrenched them all apart, but Benjamin didn't voice it to his parents. He was well aware of their feelings. He knew why they were sending him off and of the sacrifices they had made so he could go. He wished it didn't have to be this way. There was the fear of the unknown. What would he see? Whom would he meet? What would happen to him? Deep down he was afraid.

When the possibility of his leaving had come up last summer, he had wondered what he would take with him. He had to travel with as little as possible. His treasures were his tallith (prayer shawl) and the yarmulke his mother had made. He had worn them at his bar mitzvah.

His cherry trees meant much to him. If he could only take them.

"Why not?" his father asked. "Someday, in another land, maybe in America, you'll have your yard or a field. There you can have your own cherry trees."

Benjamin had saved some of the seeds. Now he brought them to his mother and she sewed them in a seam in his jacket. Then he walked out to the greening field and the cherry trees beginning to blossom. He would never see them this way again.

Late in the afternoon on Thursday, Benjamin headed for the hills, carrying a bundle of his belongings. He searched for the cave. It was a place he knew very well, having played in it with his friends many times. Those had been happy times of carefree childhood. Just inside he hid his things, covering them with rocks and some foliage growing nearby that he had picked.

Mordecai, filled with misgivings about his son's leaving, anguished and heavyhearted, closed the shop in midafternoon. In the back of the store, he sat in prayer, then went home.

Raizel, weepy-eyed, served dinner early. There wasn't much conversation this night. Each was lost in his own thoughts and fears.

Mordecai had pondered it long and hard, and thought it best the boy leave before dawn the next day, Friday. They would not have the Friday night Shabbos dinner together. Raizel was understandably upset, but when Mordecai made a decision, she, as a dutiful Jewish wife, went along with it. He usually was right more times than he was wrong.

Trying not to show his worry and concern, he called the boy. "Benjamin, *mein zuhn* [my son], someday soon, God willing, we will see each other again. God go with you."

It might take months. It might take years. They assured themselves this would happen. Each put on a brave front—for the other. Sleep evaded them all most of the night.

Very early the next morning, Mordecai went to check on the sentries at the gates. They were not out yet, but he couldn't chance going through the front entrance. Nervously he waited for Raizel and her son to say good-bye as they embraced again and again.

Then father and son left through the back door, shutting it ever so quietly, and crawled through a long secret tunnel that led to a hidden area in back of the field, covered with brush and tall grass. It was a route used by those escaping. Now Mordecai and Benjamin gave thanks because it had not yet been discovered by the enemy.

Mordecai reminded the boy once more where his escape routes would take him. If all went well, he would reach his destinations. They clung to each other, father and son, their tears blinding them. It was difficult to let go. They walked together to the spot where Benjamin crossed over toward the hills. Mordecai watched him go, then raised his eyes heavenward and prayed.

It was just a short distance more to the cave. Because he was in a hurry, Benjamin slipped and fell, the brambly bushes scratching his face and hands. Now and then he stopped to listen for any footsteps that might be coming after him.

Taking his things from their hiding place, Benjamin started up the hill to reach the narrow road running through part of the forest. He would follow it but had to stay out of sight of others on the road.

13

When he reached the top, he looked down on the settlement. He knew his parents were standing in their doorway looking up at the hills, and he felt their presence.

All that day he walked in and out of the forest, staying close to the road. When he heard anything suspicious, he hid behind the larger trees and waited.

Dusk was falling, and the air blowing down from the mountains, not too far off, was getting cooler. He hunted until he found a small clearing protected by brush and trees. Stopping just inside the area, he sat with his back against the wall of a huge rock.

For a moment Benjamin felt relaxed and it felt good to rest. He ate very little. His stomach seemed to be tied in knots. It wasn't a good feeling. The day had been long and tiring, filled with uncertainty and fear. In spite of all the difficulties, there was the excitement and anticipation of adventure in a world out there totally strange and unknown to him.

Benjamin took off his shoes, and his feet seemed to thank him. Propping his bundle into a makeshift pillow, he put his head down but couldn't sleep. He tossed and turned most of the night until every tiny pebble felt like a huge sharp-edged rock pressing into his back and legs.

It was very late when Mordecai and Raizel got to bed. They were tired. They had much to make them tired. Worrying can make you tired! Mordecai, the loving husband, tried to comfort his weeping wife, while in his mind pictures raced, pictures of what was happening to his family. He became angry; a close-knit family being forced to be separated can make one very angry.

There was hope. Always there was hope that this pain would someday translate into joy in knowing Benjamin would have a safe life, living in freedom.

Just thinking about it quieted the tumult in Mordecai's brain. Jews always hoped to be free in their own land, and for centuries when they were driven and expelled by their enemies there was the hope that kept living in the survivors: *Next year, with God's help, in Jerusalem.* Mordecai hoped for Benjamin, *Someday soon in America.*

Benjamin awoke to the chatter and squeaks of some small, curious animals. He tried to stretch some of the soreness out of his bones, without much success, but his movements sent his early morning visitors scampering.

At the town of Razekne, his destination, Benjamin was to meet his first contact of the underground. These groups or societies, as they were known, were established in many countries, cities, and villages. They formed a secret, reliable network dedicated to helping escaping Jewish travelers who had no papers or passports.

Their involvement placed them in grave danger. The groups were very selective in choosing their members. They were people who had suffered great personal losses at the hands of the government and its officials. They were willing to give their lives so others could escape. They were interested in one thing: helping others to survive the hatred of anti-Semitism.

Contact was made by secret codes, messages, or signs. Sometimes members of the underground were caught and tortured mercilessly to death, but none ever revealed the secret of the underground, for it would have put a network of thousands in jeopardy. The routes had to be kept open at all costs for the escaping Jewry.

Benjamin had been warned to be careful. There were spies everywhere. The Jew-hating peasants reported anyone or anything suspicious to the government, and the government paid them well. The successful apprehension of a Jew commanded a better bounty.

Benjamin stood ready now and, taking a last look down the valley, turned southward, following the road that would take him out of Soroki.

He hoped to cross Moldavia, wedged in between the Russian Ukraine and Romania, to the Prut River, which borders Moldavia and Romania. With help from the underground he would reach his next destination, Romania.

Benjamin could not accept rides from villagers. Enemies of the Jews were everywhere, so he had to be extremely cautious. He would have to walk most of the way, keeping off roads, going over hills and plains and through forested areas. He didn't mind, but then he had no conception of the long, arduous journey on which he was embarking. He set off like a young Columbus, only this one would travel on land.

Chapter 4

A Witness to Brutality

As a youngster, playing in the hills, Benjamin had often observed the guards at the border. There was a stone-arched bridge over a stream, with guards stationed at each end, who marched stiffly, keeping careful watch of travelers going through. Sometimes the boy saw beatings committed upon those unlucky enough to be detained for one reason or another.

Benjamin remembered, quite clearly, the day a young couple crossing were told to leave their packages and wait inside the border station. Immediately, and with tense fury, the guards ripped the bundles apart, slashing everything. They seemed to know what they were looking for. Their searched netted them a small package of tea. The couple was bringing it to the wife's mother. Because of shortages, it was forbidden to bring any food across the border.

Disobedience meant severe punishment. The tea was confiscated. Then the soldiers, following orders to make an example of the couple, had them put their right hands on the rail. One soldier held them, while another brought his sharp sword down, hacking their hands off. The hands fell below.

Benjamin, horror-stricken, put his hands over his ears, but he couldn't shut out their pitiful screams of pain.

Everyone in the village wondered, *How did the border guards know to stop this couple and search their belongings in such a violent manner?*

Later, the villagers learned the answer. The wife, talking to a friend, had mentioned her upcoming visit to her parents. She had said that for weeks there had been a shortage of tea in their town and she was bringing them half of her ration.

The friend turned out to be an informer for the government. The villagers now knew of one spy in their midst. A secret meeting was held to decide the fate of the traitor. A select few were chosen to watch her every move. She knew she was a marked woman. No one spoke to her. She became isolated in the community. Then one night she mysteriously disappeared. Government officials could not locate her. "She went away to visit relatives," was the answer to their inquiries.

16

Only the "select few" knew her fate. No one ever mentioned her again. This became a closed issue. Benjamin and the others had learned several lessons from these events. First, there was every reason to fear the government and its brutal punishments; second, family matters must be kept within the family.

Unfamiliar with the surroundings outside the village, Benjamin kept off the road, away from borders. He hoped to find his way by following the Dnestr River to Kamenka. In the square of Kamenka he could fill his water container at the fountain. He was on his way there when he saw guards standing at the gate. He turned and walked slowly away in the direction of the field, expecting at any moment to hear a shout of "Halt!" from the guards.

It had turned miserably warm, and he was hot and thirsty. He sat where the grass was tallest, hiding until the terrifying guards left their posts. The sun went down and a light breeze came up, fanning the grass, rippling through it. He lifted his face to catch it, and it made him feel better.

Benjamin watched and as soon as the guards left hurried to the fountain. It looked so inviting, he wished he could stay and wash, but it was too dangerous. Quickly he filled his container. Luck was with him; he made it back just as the two other guards took up their stations for the night.

He got as comfortable as he could on the ground, turning damp from the cooler night air. Taking his jacket from the bundle, he placed it over his shoulders and felt the pouch sewn in the sleeve. His thoughts were of his parents, and he felt comforted, a sense of calm.

Later—he didn't know how much later—he was abruptly awakened by something, a noise. His heart pounded wildly and his mouth went dry. He tried to breathe quietly, his senses alert, and listened. Not a muscle of his moved for what seemed like an eternity. All he heard was the eerie silence of the dark night.

In the early mornings, he pressed onward through low hills and brush-covered areas. During the day, he sometimes got close to villages along the way, always keeping a sharp lookout for enemy guards or soldiers in some hiding place, waiting to trap the unwary.

Steadily he plodded the miles, always looking for the landmarks that assured him he was on the right road. Late one afternoon, Benjamin was on a hill in a densely wooded thicket when he saw soldiers on horseback on the road below. They were ordered to halt almost below where Benjamin hid. Then they began combing the area, looking for someone. Once they got on the trail of someone,

17

they were like bloodhounds, searching until their prey was found. They were angry. They slashed savagely at the shrubs. Benjamin became frightened.

Are they looking for me? he wondered. He didn't know. They could be.

What if they come up here? Benjamin thought of what he could do. For a moment he had the urge to get up and run. But then they would see him. Knowing running would be foolish, he decided to stay hidden as long as he could. No matter what happened, he would not leave unless it was safe to venture forth. They kept coming higher up the slope, closer to where he sat hunched up. His teeth were clenched so tight his jaws hurt.

Then excited shouts came from some soldiers. They had found what they were looking for. A young man about sixteen or seventeen years of age, near Benjamin's age, came out trembling, terribly frightened. To Benjamin's amazement, they didn't kill him right then: some soldiers tied his hands with a rope, put a rope around his neck, and forced him to walk ahead of other soldiers on horseback. Angrily they prodded him with bayonets. His shirt was becoming bloodstained bright red where he had been cut. They then began to gallop, to go faster, and jostled him from side to side between the riders. They had him on a run, and he fell exhausted. They dragged him as the rope tightened about his neck. Then jumping down, a few struck him again and again with their bayonets.

One soldier raised his sword and cut the boy's head off. It rolled to the side of the road. Then they rode off, leaving him as a warning to others who might be contemplating escape.

Benjamin had watched some of it, turning his head away several times. The realization that the young man could have been him caused him to tremble uncontrollably. He was angered at the soldiers' cruel and heartless behavior, then angry with himself because he couldn't help. He tried to throw up but couldn't. When he was sure they were all gone, he started off in a hurry, anxious to get to his destination. More than ever he knew the importance of avoiding the guards and soldiers.

Passing a farm, he stopped and picked a few apples that had fallen near the fence. He didn't feel guilty taking them. God had provided, knowing Benjamin was hungry and without even a piece of bread. He would never forget how good the apples tasted at that moment. He savored each bite, sweet and juicy, which refreshed him and quenched his thirst. He thanked God before he ate and thanked Him after.

As Benjamin had been fortified with the bit of "heaven-sent" nourishment, his walk to the next town didn't seem so long. He stayed off the main street, carefully observing the villagers. There were no soldiers, which was unusual for even a small town, but the government could have a number of informants or members of the secret police about. This meant Benjamin would have to be extremely cautious. His intuition told him to move out of this territory quickly.

At one spot he became impatient. He had to hide and wait while a peasant took a small herd of goats down from the hill to a barn across the way. There was a field with a small vegetable patch and grapevines covered with lush green foliage. An overwhelming sense of homesickness pervaded Benjamin's whole being. He wished he were home.

He didn't belong here. He felt like what he was, an outsider, a stranger. Thoughts of home made him feel alone, but they also lifted his spirits, and he walked on with a renewed buoyancy in his step.

He had been lucky with the weather. The days were as summer days should be and getting warmer. Today, however, he traveled under a densely gray sky. Darker clouds hung low in large clumps, and off in the distance the rumble of thunder could be heard. Lightning cut huge zigzags down the center of the darkening sky and began coming at more frequent intervals while the thunder rolled in closer in his direction.

Benjamin quickened his steps toward an old barn with a thatched roof just as the rain started falling in teasing well-spaced drops. Then the rain began in earnest, its pelting in a quicker drumming sound just as he reached the barn. He was thankful to be sheltered for the night.

The soaking rain came down for two days and two nights. It came in wherever the thatched roof had been pulled away in huge pieces.

Benjamin sat up on the seat of a broken-down cart, trying to keep his feet dry despite the water coming in over the dirt floor.

Toward morning of the third day, the rain finally let up. Shivering, cold, wet, and hungry, he opened the door and scanned the field as far as his eyes could see. He saw no one, so he ventured out.

He was greatly concerned. He had traveled about twenty-five miles and should have met one of his contacts. Benjamin realized he must have taken a wrong turn at some point. Starting back, he again passed one of the villages and, on its outskirts, a church. He saw no one resembling the contact.

Now, he wondered, *where can I go? I know no one.* It was too dangerous to ask questions of anyone.

Chapter 5

Benjamin, Chaia, and Jacob

Benjamin had been coached about the different landmarks to watch for on his journey to freedom. These landmarks were guideposts to finding his way through areas that posed a danger for him. Every time he found one that enabled him to go forward, he became more sure of himself, a little more confident. There was a growing inner strength. He found he could manage on his own.

As Benjamin neared one village, he heard church bells calling to the worshipers. He headed in that direction. Then he saw it, the closed gate leading to some old buildings. He unlatched it and walked in, shutting the gate behind him. He stood, not moving, for there, leaning against the wall of a building, was a woman. In her arms she carried a basket of fruit.

He turned to walk out when he heard her speak in Russian. "Could you hold the basket for me?" she asked. She opened her shawl, and he saw the "sign."

Surprise showed in his face, but he returned the sign. No one had told him there was a possibility the contact might be a lone woman, engaged in this dangerous work.

She was called Chaia. She hurried Benjamin along the road, anxious to hear about his trip thus far and the explanation of why he was late. They walked along a road on the hill to her home in a restricted area. All the homes for Jews were dilapidated and run-down. This was an all-too-familiar sight to Benjamin.

After they had eaten, Chaia told Benjamin he would have to stay longer than planned. Word had filtered through that another person would be joining Benjamin. They were to continue the rest of the journey together. Benjamin was really happy about this. Now he would have company. He was quite satisfied to stay in one place for a few days.

Chaia and Benjamin had the opportunity to talk of several things. He told her about his family and his hope that they would be together again someday. Chaia told him how she came to be part of the underground. Benjamin learned that her husband had been taken off the street as he was returning from work. He was falsely charged with a crime he knew nothing about. There were no witnesses, no trial. He was sent away to the labor camps in Siberia for twenty-five years.

"That was nine years ago," she said.

There were no answers to her inquiries and there was no one to contact anymore. She had not been married very long when he was taken. Sometimes it was hard to remember what he looked like. She kept conjuring up his face in her mind, so as not to forget him. The days wore on with increasing agony, and the nights were lonely and long.

When the underground approached Chaia for help, she agreed without hesitation. Her life took on meaning again. Wherever she was needed she went, always eager to do whatever she could. She was part of the powerful resistance.

For the next few days Chaia walked to the village and waited, as was the underground's bidding. When she came back alone, it was with much disappointment. The following week she was anxious to start out again. A quiet rain had fallen during the night, and the morning was damp. Chaia took a jacket with her; she was sure the person she was to meet would have spent the night in the rain.

It was late in the afternoon when Benjamin saw Chaia returning with a young man. They were engaged in serious conversation, and the newcomer appeared to be quite agitated. As they came closer, Benjamin recognized her companion as Jacob, a boy about sixteen from Benjamin's settlement. He could hardly contain his joy. Now he would have some news about his parents.

Almost as soon as they greeted each other, Benjamin bombarded Jacob with a deluge of questions. "Did you see my parents? How were they? Did they talk about me? Miss me?"

But before the boy could answer, Chaia interrupted. "Let him rest, and we'll eat, then talk."

Benjamin remembered back to how he had left the village early on a Friday morning because his father had insisted. He remembered how badly he felt not having *Shabbos* dinner with his parents. He had argued, "What difference would one day make?" His parents had almost relented, but then Mordecai reiterated his concern, that Thursday night: "No, you must go tomorrow morning. Every day you stay is a dangerous one."

Jacob gave an account of what had happened. In the early dawn hours of that Sabbath morning, cossack troops, drunk with vodka and wine, had swooped down from the hills on the sleeping settlement. Merciless in their fervor of hate, they killed many in their homes, some in their beds.

Others, hearing the turmoil, came out and tried to escape but were downed by the troops on horses. The horses reared up and came down, trampling the many who fell. Cries and screams filled the air. Horrified mothers ran with their frightened children. There was no place to run to. The cossacks on horseback closed off the entrance. Others rode between the screaming, falling women and children, running their swords through them. They fell back bloody and moaning. Then death made them quiet.

The men of the settlement, many still in their nightclothes, fought to save their families from the executioners, but the villagers' weapons—sticks and pieces of broken furniture—were no match for the ferociously mad, hysterical soldiers' swords.

Many villagers were decapitated and fell on their dead families strewn in the ghetto yard. The more villagers fell, the more frenzied the soldiers became. One downed Jacob. The boy tried to beat him off, but the sword went through his shoulder and he fell unconscious. He lay there bleeding, other bodies falling on top of him. Homes and shops were ransacked and set afire.

Jacob awoke to noises near him. He could hear heavy-booted footsteps and the boisterous, noisy soldiers as they pulled at the bodies, some still writhing and twitching, and piled them on the roaring fires. The stench of burning flesh filled the air. The sky blackened with smoke borne away by the wind.

Jacob, telling of these events, had to pause several times. It was hard for him to go on. "I lay there pretending to be dead. Then I heard footsteps approaching me. I was sure someone would pull me out and throw me on the fire."

Then Jacob heard the captain's orders for the men to "Mount up. Everything will burn here!" he said. The murdering troops got back on their horses, waving their bloody swords. They were ecstatic in the day's work well done—another village of Jews annihilated.

"The government will be pleased!"

Jacob could see the captain with his blood-dripping sword held high, lead his troops out, victorious over a defenseless enemy, a small Jewish settlement, leaving it in devastation.

There were no burial plots in a cemetery, no markers in a cemetery. There wasn't even a cemetery to show there had ever been a village and in that village the family of Raizel, Mordecai, and Benjamin Rothman.

Jacob couldn't go on. His voice choked, and his shoulders shook. Telling it was living through the horror again. When he composed himself enough to continue, he told how he lay there, having a difficult time breathing, as dead bodies boxed him in.

Several times Jacob thought he heard something. It seemed to come from somewhere near him. He listened intently and heard it again—a gasp. He tried to move the body almost on top of him. As he did, he recognized it as Reb Lazer. He was badly injured, and one arm came to rest on Jacob's injured shoulder. Jacob didn't move. Then he heard Reb Lazer speak in Yiddish. He spoke haltingly, with long pauses.

"Nem de Siddurim. Nem de Siddurim. [Take the prayer books. Take the prayer books.]" Then he gave one long, torturous gasp and his arm fell lifeless from Jacob's shoulder.

Benjamin, sobbing, nodded his head. He understood about the prayer books. When the government banned religious teachings and religious books for the Jews of the village, the men had held a secret meeting. A way to save some books and continue the Hebrew learning was decided upon.

From the back of one of the houses at the end of the court nearest to the hills a secret tunnel was dug. It took a few years to complete. The dirt from the tunnel was carried out little by little and deposited near bushes or in the hills or the forest. It had to be done cautiously so as not to arouse suspicion.

The walls of the tunnel were shored up with wood from the forest and rocks. Small trees were chopped for firewood and stored outside the cottages. Every home was called on to contribute wood. The tunnel had preference; it was the first priority.

Inside the tunnel a shelf was built against a wall. Prayer books forbidden by the government were kept there. Each book was wrapped in a cloth. If trouble came to the village, anyone escaping was to go through the tunnel and take at least one siddur with him to where others could study and learn. This was of importance, survival of the Jewish religion. Tyrants in the government could kill many things, but they couldn't kill this spark. It stayed alive, to ignite somewhere else.

Jacob had waited, stiff from staying in one position without moving. He extricated himself from the death around him and crawled to the house, which was still smoldering. He entered the tunnel and crept along the wall, feeling his way to the shelf. He took two prayer books. He wanted to save more but knew it was too dangerous. The books had been wrapped, prepared for just such an emergency. He stayed in the tunnel overnight.

In the morning he slid out from the dirt into the field and

24

stopped to hide in the grasses until he could get to the river. He lay there anguished and in pain. His mind still couldn't comprehend the carnage that had taken place.

Jacob cleansed his wound as best he could. He didn't take time to rest—it was urgent that he get away from this area that once was his home.

As Jacob had recounted the tragedy, Benjamin closed his eyes. Tears ran down his cheeks. He called, "Oy Mamaleh! Oy Tahtaleh! [Oh, little Mother! Oh, little Father!]" He kept repeating it over and over. He was in such pain, overwhelming pain.

Chaia hovered in the background, not knowing what to do to help them in their grief. "Such a tragedy, such a tragedy." And then she'd interject, "Oy vey! Oy vey!"

After a little while she brought food. It was the only thing she could think to do. "Eat something. You'll feel better."

That night Benjamin's thoughts were of his parents. He lay there going over the pogrom. He tried to picture his parents, his father trying to shield his mother, as the soldiers came after them. Benjamin prayed they didn't suffer, that if death had to come, it had come swiftly.

In his young life Benjamin had seen the government's hate manifest itself in many ways in and around the area where he lived, but his parents had always been there with him. On this journey of escape to freedom he had seen man's inhumanity to man in the brutality at the border and in the capture and death of the young boy trying to escape. These were terrible acts of violence to witness, but even though Benjamin was far away from his parents, he had felt they were with him. Now they were gone, wiped off the face of the earth. A chill pervaded his whole being.

Guilt consumed him. If he had not gone away, maybe he could have helped them. Then he remembered why he was here. His parents had worried about the possibility of just such a tragedy occurring and had shown foresight, courage, and unselfish love in helping Benjamin go to a safer place, to a better life, to freedom!

At that time he didn't know they were a family of history. A family without history is a tree without roots. Mordecai and Raizel were the tree, and Benjamin was one of the young spreading roots!

Chaia was well aware of the risk in having one escapee staying with her. Now there was a heightened sense of danger, having two. Jacob especially worried her. He carried the forbidden prayer books. These jeopardized the lives of both young men even more. Word in the settlement was that soldiers were in town searching for new-comers who might be escapees.

With great misgiving, Chaia got the boys up while it was still dark out. She wished they could have stayed a bit longer, as the boys were tired and bereaved. They set off with Jacob hidden in the hay in the cart. Benjamin sat up front watching for soldiers.

Chaia tried to hurry the old horse along while silently she prayed the underground would be there in time to pick up these two. While they were with her, they were her charges and she was responsible for their safety, but she would worry when they were gone.

When it was time for Chaia to take leave of them, it was more difficult, since Benjamin had been with her longer. She had been warm and kind, and Benjamin felt close to her. For Chaia, too, there was always the pain of letting go. For a while he had helped fill the void in her life.

As she had said to Benjamin when he tried to thank her, "God provides. He lets us do good for each other."

When they arrived at the boys' new route, Chaia got down from the cart. She kissed and embraced them both, wishing them, "Mazel [Good luck]," in their new homes. They didn't want to leave her, but it was time to go. She was anxious for them to start, to get to their new contact.

Chaia watched from the road until they were gone from sight, headed into a thick-wooded area. She got back in the cart and fixed the hay to hide any telltale signs of her "visitors."

Now, going back, Chaia didn't hurry. She let the horse plod its way slowly. Thoughts of her life came to her. From the corners of her mind came pictures of her husband, their wedding, and friends. She smiled; she had not thought about these things for a long time.

Her life was far from a good life; it was an everyday struggle to survive her loneliness and the hate about her. She was happy when the "visitors" came and she got them off safely. It was a tremendously satisfying feeling. Something right had been accomplished, and she had been instrumental in its achievement. It was important to her. It was her reason for living.

She was nearing home, lost in thought and did not see the soldiers until it was too late. She tried to turn the cart around, but they were already galloping toward her. They were fierce-looking, barbaric in their every thought, and they struck fear in her heart.

She was brought back to her house. There were soldiers outside, too. She couldn't think of what had alerted them. She knew the punishment would be severe.

The brutal soldiers pushed her down from the cart, and she fell hard into the dirt road. The rocks skinned her face on one side and her hands. A neighbor would later tell of Chaia's punishment and what transpired.

The soldiers pulled her up by her hair and tried to get information from her. They then ransacked her house and set it afire.

Chaia had once told a member of the underground, "If I am ever caught and tortured, the faces of all those who escaped will keep marching through my mind. I'll never tell!"

She was tortured but refused to give out any information about the boys or where she had taken them. They couldn't be followed.

Benjamin learned Chaia had been found beaten to death, with her eyes gouged out. Her body was left in the road, a warning to the underground. Brave Chaia, gentle and warm, had given her life so Benjamin and others could escape for a chance at a better life. Benjamin never forgot her.

Chapter 6

The Fisherman

Benjamin and Jacob had traveled from Faleshty to the Prut River, where they had to find a way across. They stopped at a fishing village where boats of all sizes were coming in or going out.

Peasants were working unloading fish, and boats already relieved of their cargoes were docked and their fishing nets hung up to dry. Peasant women hustled about helping their men load fish into baskets. Then the women carried the baskets up to the market nearby. A group of women sat on one dock socializing while they repaired a huge net spread out before them. The nets dried quickly in the bright morning sun. The day would be warmer.

Benjamin paused near a boat and watched as waves lapped against it. It bobbed from side to side, hitting the dock with crunching sounds. Benjamin's mind was caught up in the sounds of the busy hubbub of the village. It looked peaceful enough, as if there were no hate here, but that wasn't so. For certainly there were spies scrutinizing everyone.

Benjamin took notice of the fishermen sitting near the boats. He walked slowly up and down the road. This was dangerous; he couldn't be careless, but he was following instructions and was on the alert. He passed one fisherman, then another. They could be observing him. Nonchalantly he stopped to pick a few pebbles and skimmed them into the river.

An elderly fisherman sat mending his net, plying his needle with skillful hands. He seemed totally engrossed in his work. Once he glanced up as Benjamin came by as if he had suddenly become aware of someone walking back and forth. With great care he set down his needle and net. He stood up and opened the top of his shirt as if to cool off. Benjamin's eyes brightened with recognition of the "sign." Eagerly he approached the fisherman's boat and inquired in Russian, "Is there anyone here who can take us up the river?"

"Da! Da!" The fisherman nodded his head. He stood up and scanned the people about. There were no soldiers, which meant there might be a government informer. He motioned the boys into the boat and asked for the fee, a few kopecks. Benjamin counted the pieces one by one as he placed them in the hand of the fisherman. If anyone was watching, Benjamin appeared to be just a paying customer.

Before they could get seated, the man took the boat out. In Yiddish he apologized for the rush. "One never knows where the *tyvel* [devil, slang for informer] is."

The man, Benjamin learned, was called Misha. He confided that wasn't his real name. He lived in the village as a Gentile, a *goy,* a Russian peasant. He went to their gatherings that denounced Jews. He had to take part in their Jew-baiting propaganda.

Because his wife and child had been murdered in a pogrom, Misha became part of the underground. His work was most important. Here he could help escapees across the river into Romania. To do this, he became a fisherman with his own boat, and he had a pulse on what was happening with the peasants. To the villagers, he seemed not to be a very good fisherman. He didn't catch too many fish, and they didn't mind that he earned a few kopecks when he ferried peasants who wanted to go up the river to another village.

When his passengers were his countrymen (those escaping), Misha took them out away from other boats and hurried them straight across to safe points on the other side. There the underground in Romania took over.

His life was a lonesome one. He longed for his own kind, other Jews. Jews here knew him as a peasant *goy.* Sometimes Jews passed him and he heard them speaking Yiddish. His heart leapt with the sweetness of it, but he had to walk on as if he didn't understand it.

He was a stranger here. His commitment was to work here. Hundreds had been helped across safely. Every time he took one across safely, he thanked God.

It was warm with the sun beating down. Benjamin removed his jacket. Misha took them quite a ways up the river and across. They disembarked at what Misha said was a "good place." They were in Romania.

Benjamin couldn't believe he had reached one country his parents had wanted him to be in. He thanked Misha.

"You don't have to thank me," Misha said in Yiddish. "I'm doing it for my wife, my child, and for myself." He was reluctant to part from the boys. There hadn't been a "landsman" for him to take across for many weeks. He had worried the escape route had been discovered. He told the boys, "I feel good talking to landsmen in the language of my parents, my childhood. I miss it."

The two youths were to separate at this point. Misha showed Jacob where to pick up his route, with instructions on where he was to meet his contact. Benjamin would continue in a westerly direction to Iasi (Ya'she).

"We've said so many good-byes and left so many friends. It's always sad to leave a friend," Jacob said.

Benjamin embraced Jacob. "Maybe we will see each other again."

The young men went on in different directions. Misha watched them go as he had watched so many others. He wondered what their lives would be like in the new places. These boys were young and full of hope. Misha wanted their lives to be good.

Misha turned his boat around and headed back to spend more days watching, waiting, and hoping there would be more refugees. Each one Misha took across safely to him symbolized a victory over the oppressors.

Please, God, he prayed, *let there be more!*

Chapter 7

A New Beginning

Benjamin came to Romania about 1892, when its ruler was Carol I. It was a time when the country had been undergoing changes and new economic developments. It was known there were more work opportunities there for Jews. To take advantage of this, many Jews escaping Russia came to Romania.

These changes had been taking place gradually. Romania had been under the sovereignty of the Turks. The provisional government in Romania searched for someone to rule them. They chose Prince Karl, a German and a commissioned officer in the army stationed in Berlin.

The German prince's presence in Romania was illegal, according to the Turks, and they massed their troops along the Danube. And so began the Russo-Turkish wars. Karl led the Romanian and Russian troops in a decisive battle in these wars. His reward was to be independence for Romania.

First, Romania had to mend her anti-Semitic ways, which had been a problem to the Western powers. Jews had been denied many rights, including the right to vote. Landowners and peasants hated Jews, constantly pressuring the government to enact harsher restrictions against these people, whose only crime was being Jews!

For the prince, the anti-Semitic problem was one of enormous magnitude. He feared the rich Jews of Western Europe would use their influence to stop the capital he desperately needed after the war to further develop his country from reaching it.

Romania was forced in this way to grant privileges to Jews, but whatever was done was done grudgingly. The country's department for naturalization obeyed in one way: they gave the vote to families of men who had fought for Romania in the Russo-Turkish wars and survived. However, there weren't many, as Romanian Jewish soldiers had been taken out of their regiments and placed in the front lines, the first to be killed.

Prince Karl had to give back Bessarabia to Russia and complied, somewhat, with the demand for Jews, then proclaimed Romania an independent kingdom and at his coronation, changed his German name, Karl, to Carol I of Romania. The year was 1881.

He became very wealthy with taxes paid to the crown, while the peasants became poorer. They rose up in angry revolt. Uprisings and revolts became more frequent and grew in their brutality.

When Benjamin arrived things were not good, but a little better than in Russia.

Benjamin's contacts brought him to the Schlosser family in Iasi. Abe had a small tailor shop, where he repaired clothes. He always found a little work to do, but there wasn't much money. Still it was ample for Abe and his wife, Hannah.

When they were asked if they could take Benjamin, they said, "Yes." It was another mouth to feed, but they would manage. "It's a necessary thing. We have to help our people. It's a mitzvah," Abe said, discussing it with Hannah.

Benjamin felt strange at first. This was a new land, a new language, new people, and a new home—a whole new world for him. Who could blame him for the many times he felt alone, when his thoughts reverted back to his home in Russia and his parents?

It was at these times the boy would become quiet. He would do his work but wouldn't say too much. Abe and Hannah were very patient and understanding. They knew it was more difficult for the young boy to accept them than it was for them to accept him. They had already taken him to their hearts. To Abe, Benjamin was like a son. Abe had taken him into the shop and was teaching him the art of tailoring. He would learn it well and become self-supporting.

Hannah was a handsome, plump woman with big blue-gray eyes that were sad. A religious woman, she spent her days in prayers and tears, wondering why the child she and Abe desired had been denied them. This was the great sorrow of her life. When Benjamin arrived, things began to change. All her smothered maternal instincts found a release. Taking care of Benjamin became one of her priorities, and she began to feel fulfilled as a woman.

Abe was well aware of the difference Benjamin had brought to their home. His Hannah's eyes were smiling again, and when she prayed, there were tears, but they were tears of happiness. Her prayers had been answered, not as she had hoped, but God moves in mysterious ways.

Benjamin, too, thanked God for bringing him to the Schlossers—to Abe, a gentle, caring man, and Hannah, warm-hearted and kind. Benjamin enjoyed his work, and he helped Abe and Hannah in any way he could.

The week went by quickly, and when Friday came they all looked forward to *Shabbos*. It was good to see smiling faces. Hannah lighted the candles, and Abe and Benjamin joined in the kiddush. They sat and enjoyed the dinner Hannah had prepared so carefully. Benjamin loved the roast chicken with *mamaliga* (a type of cornmeal). Hannah beamed as the boy ate with a good a appetite.

"Ah gesundt awf dine kopf [good health to you]." Hannah was one of God's happiest creatures!

The first year passed, and then the second. Benjamin was becoming impatient. He loved his home and the Schlossers, but he wanted a shop of his own and his own home, and Abe agreed. It was time for him to get married and settle down.

Matchmakers often took it upon themselves to put people together. An eligible young man in the village gave them something to talk about. Malke, the matchmaker, came to Abe. She would try to find a suitable wife for Benjamin. It wasn't too long before she bustled herself in with the name of a young woman: Slovie Bregman.

Everyone in the village knew the friendly Slovie. She was a pretty, petite young woman. The matchmaker extolled all Slovie's virtues. She was a *balabosteh* (a good housekeeper). She would make a home—a home! She would be a wonderful wife and someday a good mother, "God willing!"

Abe and Hannah listened. They wanted the best for Benjamin, their Benjamin. Finally Abe spoke. "With *alleh mallehs* [all these virtues], there must be a *chasoorim* [fault]."

Malke nodded. There was a drawback, an important point to consider. There would be a dowry, but not a large one. The family was poor.

"Oh." Abe wasn't too happy. Benjamin deserved a girl with a nice dowry. The young man had struggled; he had gone through much. Abe wanted him to at least have a good start in life.

The matchmaker knit her brows together. She didn't want to lose this match. It meant money to her. She had to convince the Schlossers that Slovie's wonderful personality and character outweighed any larger dowry.

The matchmaker spoke to the Bregmans of Benjamin's ambition. He was a hard worker and wanted to have his own shop. He was a good, religious young man and came from a refined family. Malke told the Bregmans, "Any girl would be proud to call him husband."

The Schlossers and the Bregmans were then left to consider the proposals. A most happy Malke called on the families as preliminaries were set. Benjamin and the Schlossers were to come Friday night

33

for *Shabbos* dinner. The couple and their families would meet to see if all the matchmaker had promised was true.

Everyone knew that to get a fee some matchmakers could be quite deceitful. They exaggerated so that the plainest women were always "beauties"—none were ever fat or had faults. Men were always tall, dark, and handsome, never bald or fat or old. They were always "*shain vi de zin* [beautiful like the sun]." Many times there were disappointments on both sides because of this. Many times the marriages went forward depending on whether the dowry was a substantial one.

All week long the anticipation of the meeting caused anxieties in both families. Friday came. The Bregman family had been busy cleaning, cooking, and baking. Now they were ready to receive the company.

Slovie waited at the curtained window and saw them coming up the street. She saw a tall young man. He had hair on his head; he wasn't bald. To this she breathed a sigh of relief. She liked the looks of him, and in her girlish heart she hoped he would like her, too.

The families sat prim and proper, each putting their best foot forward. Mrs. Bregman's round face flushed with the anticipation of a bride-to-be in the family as she kindled the *Shabbos* candles. Slovie's eyes were on her mother, but her thoughts were on someday having her own home, lighting her own *Shabbos* candles with a husband. She could feel her face blushing and looked down at her hands.

Benjamin glanced across the table just then and thought he had never seen such a fine young woman. Slovie's brown hair had golden glints in it, and when she looked up her green eyes shone with the reflection of the candle glow.

The dinner went well. Complimented on the food, Mrs. Bregman made sure to volunteer that Slovie had helped and was a wonderful cook. Mrs. Schlosser nodded her head in approval. The young folk sat quietly listening but couldn't enter the conversation. They sat as plans for their future lives were going forward.

Slovie's father announced what her dowry would be: First, there were two down pillows and a down quilt, all made by her mother. The *puch* (down) feathers had been taken from white ducks and meticulously cleaned. The articles were stitched with the finest hand-sewn stitches. She had her traditional pair of candlesticks. There were sheets and towels, all made by her mother and Slovie. Proudly Mr. Bregman told everyone what a fine seamstress Slovie was.

It was not a rich dowry. The Bregmans were a poor family, but rich in having their daughter, Slovie. They spoke of her as their "diamond."

The *shidduch* (match) was made. The parents gave each other *mazel tov* (congratulations) and kissed their offspring, who were now shyly smiling.

Chapter 8

The Newlyweds

The May day dawned bright and the sun shone warmly in that year of 1894. Slovie was eighteen and Benjamin twenty when they were married. It was a small wedding with the matchmaker, Malke, as the honored guest and Slovie's parents, the Schlossers, and friends of both families.

The excited bride looked lovely in a beautiful dress her mother had made, and the nervous bridegroom was handsome as they stood under the *chupa* (canopy) and listened to the rabbi's chanting of the wedding service. Bride and groom drank wine from the same cup, and the wedding ceremony concluded with the groom stomping on a glass that had been covered with a cloth and placed on the floor. Benjamin stomped down hard and everyone heard the glass break.

"This," said the rabbi, "at a wedding, a happy occasion, reminds us of the sadness of the destruction of our temple in Jerusalem."

Then everyone sang "Groom and Bride, *Mazel Tov*," keeping time by clapping their hands. There was much hugging and kissing, and some were so happy they cried.

The matchmaker, Malke, sat beaming. She had done a good job putting these two together. She was extremely proud of herself. She had come to the wedding to enjoy herself, but she was also carefully observing the guests. In her mind she was already matchmaking. There were some unlikely pairs, but she had faith. Sometimes she had to work miracles. Folding her arms, she thought to herself, *Ah, dahnken Gott* [thank God]. There was more work for her to do. She would be busy!

After the wedding, Benjamin and Slovie stayed with her parents for a little while. The couple had made plans to move to Vaslui, about forty miles away. Benjamin wanted to open his own shop, and the area here couldn't support two tailors. The village of Vaslui needed one.

Vaslui was in a part of Romanian territory that was called Moldavia. Moldavia had two parts. The northern part, the richer part, was called Bessarabia and was coveted by Russia, who sent her troops back and forth across this area. The two countries Russia and Romania were constantly warring over Bessarabia. The Moldavians, mostly Romanians, were often ruled by Russia.

The Prut River with its black waters was the border between Russia and Romania. The lands for miles was lush, green, and fertile. Vaslui was situated in the midst of this. There were many restricted areas for Jews. In one of these areas were rows of small wooden cottages. They had high-pitched thatched roofs. Their steep pitch helped the rainwater drain off. A few pots were always kept there to catch the water. These cottages with dilapidated gates and fences made up what was the main street. There were usually one or two rooms in the houses.

Benjamin and Slovie lived in a very small two-room home. The entrance was made into the middle room, or kitchen, heated by an earthenware wood-burning stove. On one side was the family room and on the other a small space used as a storeroom.

The small family room was partitioned off by a curtain Slovie had made. This was Benjamin's shop. Abe had given him some equipment to start with—shears, needles, some cloth, and a good supply of strong thread. It was enough to start with. Benjamin was young, ambitious, and an optimist. He was a hard worker and was sure he would do well.

Benjamin could do anything he set his mind to. Whatever was needed he made. He'd plan it in his head, then go to work on it. Soon there was the finished product. He made a wooden table, two wooden benches, and their bed. Slovie was so happy. Benjamin could hear her singing as she went about their home.

The bed was set up in the other part of the family room. On it Slovie had placed part of her dowry—sheets, pillows, and the quilt. It looked so comfortable. A wooden mantel or shelf was attached to the wall near the stove. Slovie had set her candlesticks on the mantel. On the table she had placed a bowl. Both were gifts from her mother.

Slovie and Benjamin were excited newlyweds in their first home. It was a place of their own in which the couple were learning about each other.

Benjamin rented the house but had to pay a tax on a small lot in back. It was the only way he could get the cottage. The tax made things a bit difficult. He would have to work longer hours to meet the extra expense. He also hoped to have a little time to plant a few vegetables. He wanted to plant potatoes and a few cabbages to ease the food shortage.

The following spring, Benjamin planted two cherry trees. He felt settled, at home. He had a sense of belonging. That was a feeling that had eluded him for a long time.

In summer the streets in the area were dusty, and when it rained they were deep in mud. Fields of flowers stretched around the village. It was a beautiful place, but it couldn't hide the poverty of these restricted areas. Benjamin tended his garden and was anxious to dig up the potatoes and cabbages and store them for the winter.

He awoke one morning to find peasants had come in the night and taken most of the crop. He was lucky to salvage some of it, for which he gave thanks. *Never mind,* he told himself. *Next year I will grow them again.*

He wouldn't let it discourage him. It angered him. He'd worked hard and needed the food. Next year they might take the crops again, but that was part of the harassment a Jew had to live with. The hate manifested itself in many ways! Bands of thugs roamed and looted homes, shops, and gardens. The government encouraged the anti-Semitic outbreaks.

Chapter 9

Life in Vaslui

When Benjamin first opened his shop, there wasn't much business. He sat there every day for almost a week—no one came in. Helping Abe in the store was one thing, but taking the step of opening his own shop took courage. He knew that if it took hard work and confidence in his ability as a tailor, he could do it.

"It takes time," Benjamin told Slovie. She worried because she didn't want him to get discouraged. She would soon learn that wasn't Benjamin's way.

The day he got his first customer was something to celebrate. A distraught wife came in with a pair of her husband's trousers. She had been sewing a button on a back pocket, and while she was trying to cut the thread the scissors slipped, cutting the pants. She was beside herself, as it was Friday and the pants were needed for *Shabbos.*

"My husband," she said, "will be very angry. He'll kill me." Her Yiddish became very dramatic. "He'll yell. All the neighbors will hear." She was agitated and kept wringing her hands. "Zit zahn a shande! [It will be a shame!]" She'd be embarrassed.

Benjamin knew her husband wouldn't kill her. He might be furious and holler. The husband obviously was boss in his house, or she wouldn't have been so frightened.

Benjamin calmed her down and said he would try to fix them. She would have to come back later.

Benjamin went to work with infinite patience, sewing with such fine stitches that when he was finished the cut looked as if it had been interwoven. The woman came back and could not find the place where the cut had been. She paid him and was so grateful. Over and over she told him what wonderful work he did.

Benjamin came to show Slovie his first earnings. "I think I saved a marriage today." He told her the story, and they both laughed. This was their start.

Word began spreading about Benjamin's fine tailoring. Soon he got more business from his area. He was an honest man and didn't overcharge. When he earned a little extra, he would buy a small fur and make a cap, muff, or collar for a coat.

Benjamin was happy in his work. He loved his wife. They were in a country where things were not good for Jews, things could have been better. Still he was thankful he was in Romania, not Russia!

Many times he thought of his parents, Mordecai and Raizel. He wished they were here to share in his happiness. He knew they would have approved of his life. The knowledge of that made him feel good.

In the fall of the year, when Benjamin had made a supply of caps, vests, and collars, he would rent a stall at the bazaar and sell some of the pieces. He was so pleased. These were things he had made.

People commented on his creative patterns. Carefully he would cut the pieces of fur and work them into beautiful designs. It took infinite patience, and when he finished a piece it gave him tremendous satisfaction. He was kept busy, with the vegetable patch, the shop, and doing the fur pieces.

Then, with a special gladness in his heart, Benjamin made a cradle. His Slovie was pregnant with their first child. Slovie loved the cradle. She complimented Benjamin again and again, "Benjamin, my husband, you have golden hands." It was plain to see she adored him. She wondered how she came to be so lucky to have him for her husband.

Benjamin's joy was boundless. He watched Slovie as their child grew in her. He had never seen his wife look so beautiful. Benjamin was sure he was the luckiest man in the world. He thanked God many times for all his blessings.

On July 15, 1895, their daughter, Chaika (Clara), was born. She was a beautiful child. Benjamin named her after Chaia, the woman in the underground who had given her life for him.

The Bregmans came to visit for Rosh Hashana. Like all grandparents, they wanted to see that first grandchild, and of course they also wanted to see how Slovie and Benjamin were.

Slovie and her mother prepared the holiday dinner. The Bregmans had brought some food. It was the first holiday with the baby. Slovie lighted the candles, Benjamin said the kiddush over the wine, and then they all ate and enjoyed the dinner, laughing and talking, happy to be together. A family together, what a warm, wonderful feeling. The Bregmans were beaming. They could see Slovie and Benjamin were happy. What else could parents want?

The Bregmans stayed for three days, and then the good-byes were difficult. It was a long way to come, but the Bregmans said they would come again, God willing.

Slovie and Benjamin were proud parents. Slovie spent much time with Clara. Then, when Clara was five, a brother, Avram, was born. The Rothmans were a happy family. Benjamin had a son to carry on the family name. What else could a father want?

Benjamin worked harder trying to make things better for his family. Every day of the week was filled with dreariness, hard work, and struggle. Then there came the wonderful anticipation of the Sabbath. "Remember to keep the Sabbath holy," as it said in the Fourth Commandment.

The family looked forward to Friday and preparing for this wonderful time for them. *Shabbos* was as important to them as life itself. During the week, Slovie managed to save a few special delights, to set them aside for *Shabbos*—a little fruit, ingredients for a cake, a little cherry preserves. The house was spotlessly clean and shiny.

Clara would help her mother set the table with the cloth used only for *Shabbos* and holidays. The candlesticks, shiny and bright, were set with ever so much care on the table.

Slovie would bring the wonderful *challah* (bread) and cover it with the embroidered cloth she had made. Then she called them when all was ready. Covering her lovely brown hair with a kerchief, she stood there, her family's adoring eyes on her.

She moved her hands above the lighted tapers, chanting the age-old blessing over the candlesticks. Then, taking her hands from her delicate flushed face, she looked lovingly at her little family. "Good *Shabbos*," she said, and they answered, "Good *Shabbos!*"

Slovie was a queen in a household of Israel. The Sabbath candles' flame was their symbol of hope.

Then Benjamin, who had thrown off his weekday worries and washed and dressed in his Sabbath clothes, poured the wine. He chanted the kiddush, sanctifying the fruit of the vine. Slovie brought in the dinner.

They ate and talked and laughed—Benjamin, the tired father; Slovie, the warm-hearted wife and mother; and Clara and Avram, contented, loved, and loving children. They looked forward to the Sabbath, the day of rest.

Shabbos peace descended on the Rothman home.

41

Chapter 10

Young Clara

Romania was beautiful. There were flowers everywhere. In the springtime the meadows and fields were carpets of green grass and white and pink crocuses dotted the land. Toward summer there was an abundance of flowers of all hues.

Clara was a lovely child, bright-eyed and rosy-cheeked, with shiny medium brown hair that she wore in two thick, long braids. A happy child, full of laughter, she played with her friends and her mother, oblivious to the poverty surrounding her. She was a child of joy and sunshine.

Slovie loved to watch her child as she laughed and played barefoot in these fields. This was where she enjoyed picking the flowers and painstakingly would braid them into rings for her fingers and circlets, large and small, for her hair. When her playing was finished, she made sure to bring these beauties of nature home to her mother. There was a close bond between mother and child. Clara was sure there was no one as good or beautiful as her mother.

When the youngster was old enough, she attended the one-room schoolhouse near the ghetto area. The days spent there were some of the happiest in her young life. The schoolgirl was an attentive, good student and was always saddened when the school day ended. She stood in awe of the teachers because to her young mind they were special. They knew everything. She grew up with great respect for them.

Clara walked the long distance to school in all kinds of weather. Most of the time she walked barefoot, except in winter, carrying her shoes buttoned together and slung over her shoulder. At school she put the shoes on, and after they were taken off again. This was to save them as much as possible. Shoes were a luxury, and there was little or no money to repair them.

At school Clara learned to read and write the Romanian language, much of which had originated from Latin when the Romans were the country's conquerors. At home, the family spoke Yiddish and Hebrew, but Romanian had to be spoken outside the home. Any shopping outside the ghetto was done in the Romanian language and the money counted in Romanian.

Clara mastered it, learning to count to 100: *unu, doia, trei, patre, cinci, sase, sapte, opti, nana, zece, unu spre zece, doia spre zece,* etc.

Suddenly a great calamity befell the community. To quiet the demands of the rebelling peasants, new laws were enacted forbidding Jewish children to attend school.

That week Clara came to school bringing all her books, as she had been told to do. The teacher and some of the students (no Jews) collected all the Jewish children's books, and then these children were told not to come to school anymore and dismissed.

As Clara stooped down to take her shoes off, one of the peasant children hit Clara on the head. As Clara raised her face, the child spat on her. Clara saw the teacher turn away. The teacher had seen it but ignored it. Clara had revered that teacher; now she became very angry. As the few Jewish children were leaving, the class began chanting, "Jew, go home. Jew, go home." Clara began to cry as she hurried home. That was her first taste of anti-Semitism, and it left its indelible mark in her memory.

When she got home, she wanted to know, "Why?"

Benjamin tried to explain the situation, much as his parents had done with him. He had been anguished and had come to understand their pain at that time. Now he was feeling this pain, too, along with the frustrations of seeing unjust acts perpetrated against those he loved—now his child. It angered him knowing there wasn't anything he could do about it. That utter feeling of helplessness, that was the worst of it!

For Clara, not being able to attend school in the days that followed was a harsh reality. It took its toil of her as she tried to fill the former school hours with other things. She missed her books and played school by herself, writing and rewriting some of the lessons she remembered.

Slovie began to teach Clara how to knit and crochet and embroider. Being cut off from school learning, something that had been so important to her, left a void in her life. She missed being with her school friend Ileana, a peasant girl who lived near the ghetto.

Clara stood at the window enviously watching her classmates going to school. Many made faces at her. When Ileana walked by with other peasant children, she looked at Clara out of the corner of her eye, then walked on, not acknowledging her. Clara would leave the window dejected, not comprehending. When Ileana was alone, she smiled and waved at Clara. Once Ileana stopped to talk to her, furtively watching to see if anyone saw her.

"My parents won't let me play with you because you're Jewish. I'll come to see you anyway," Ileana added defiantly.

Ileana did come. The girls played in the back or in the fields where they couldn't be seen. The two friends, Jew and Gentile, were happy in the short intervals they spent together. Young as they were, they were saddened at the adverse circumstances that kept them apart.

One day, Ileana confided, "My father is angry with the Jews. He says they take work from our people. He is constantly scolding and threatening me because of you, Clara."

This hurt Clara. She, too, was frank and open with her friend. "My father thinks we shouldn't see each other. He says it is too dangerous for us and our families."

On Ileana's birthday Clara gave her a beautiful lace collar she had crocheted. It was something she had just learned to do. Ileana cried, "It's beautiful, Clara! I'll keep it forever!" Then she hid the gift in her pocket and started home.

"Maybe someday you can come to my house," she said wistfully.

Every now and then Clara and Ileana would see each other at the river when their mothers did the laundry. Sometimes they played together. Most of the time they had to stay with their own groups.

The village of Vaslui was halfway between Iasi and Bulad, on a tributary of the Moldavia River. It wasn't a very big river; still it was the lifeblood of the villagers. An open ditch of water flowed from it, providing water for the households. Fowl and livestock drank here.

The women in a group took their laundry to the river. They took turns watching for the enemy or other troublemakers. Clara and the other children played in the water, close to shore, while Clara's mother and the other women pounded the clothes on rocks. Clara would help her mother carry the wet clothes back to their home to dry. On warm, sunny days, the clothes were dried on rocks and tree branches.

Coming to the river to wash clothes was a social event. Women exchanged bits of news of the village and people. They told of new cooking tips and new ideas for stretching the little food they had. Someone always came up with a new way to fix *mamaliga*, a cornmeal used extensively in every household.

It was hard work pounding the clothes, and the women were usually tired at the end of the day after the long walks home. Still, it was also a day of enjoyment for Clara and Slovie to spend this time together at the river.

Chapter 11

Slovie Becomes Ill

For awhile all seemed to be going well for the family. Both parents were so proud that they now had a daughter and a son. To Benjamin it was an overwhelming feeling; he had a son to carry on his name, the name of his father. Benjamin couldn't describe it, except it was almost a religious feeling. He had what every Jewish father wanted, a kaddish.

Clara was thrilled with the baby brother. "So small, so small," she said over and over, as she touched his tiny fingers. Being with him for even a little while was a pleasurable way to spend the time she had spent in school, which she missed.

Benjamin looked forward to mealtimes with his little family circle at the end of the day. They were good times. Here in their home with their family, Slovie and Benjamin were content—poor but content.

Then Slovie fell ill. She had never fully recovered from the birth of Avram. She tired easily and had to rest often. Benjamin thought this was because of the added work of caring for the baby, so he made every effort to help her as much as he could. She didn't respond to the medication and became progressively worse. Benjamin was in deep despair.

It soon fell to Clara to help her mother. It started with small things, like getting something for the baby. Then food had to be prepared. Clara learned how to cook in a most unconventional manner. She would bring a pot to her mother's bed, then bring the ingredients. Slovie would tell her, "Take a handful of this, a pinch of that, and four or six glasses of water, put it on the stove, and watch until it boils down to here." Then she'd show Clara where that point was on the pot.

Of course, there were accidents and mistakes, but each had the patience of Job. Soon Clara was making some tasty dishes. Her parents were so proud of her. She developed a real love for cooking. She was always intrigued by the finished product resulting from a mixture of different ingredients.

Slovie loved this child of hers and was quite aware of the girl's concern for her. There was a strong bond between these two. Clara loved to come sit on the bed just to be near her mother. It was her favorite spot.

Slovie often told Clara what a wonderful child she was and what a great help to her. They had many quiet moments together. Slovie, often restless, loved to have Clara brush her long hair. She closed her eyes and felt so relaxed.

"Oh, Mamaleh," she would tell her, "that feels so good."

Slovie called Clara "Mamaleh" (little mother) because she was the little mother in the house. Sometimes when Slovie felt better and was having less pain, they would talk for just a little while. When Slovie closed her eyes, Clara knew she was tired. The conversation ended, but Clara stood near the bed and watched her mother. She was very sensitive to her mother's pain and so many times wished it would disappear.

Clara wanted her mother to be up and well and everything to be wonderful again. It all seemed so long ago. Clara had made so many wishes, but nothing happened. Slovie was an invalid now, spending all of her time in bed.

Slovie hated the control this illness had on all their lives. She realized what it was doing to Clara. It was robbing her of her childhood. Slovie was distressed and angry with herself for being the cause of the family's anguish and pain.

When she voiced this to Benjamin, he tried to quiet her restlessness and soothe her anger. He knew it was worry for the family that was taking its toll of Slovie, as well as her illness.

Tenderhearted Clara would have done anything that was asked of her, because she felt whatever she was doing was helping her mother get well. She heard her father say many times, "Slovie, when you feel better we'll do this." To Clara this meant her mother would be well. It was just a matter of time. She had never known about illness before.

It was difficult to get a Romanian doctor to come to the ghetto. They charged big fees but refused to come. Benjamin was hopeful one of these doctors could make Slovie well. At last the day came when the tall, stern-faced doctor, with his little black satchel, arrived. The children were told to go outdoors.

Benjamin looked on as the doctor carefully examined Slovie. She looked so pale and gaunt it was like a stab to Benjamin's heart. The doctor gently sat her up and listened to her heart. After what seemed like an eternity, he closed his medical bag. Benjamin went out to the shop, and the doctor followed.

Slovie, quite weary, lay back. She heard them conversing in low

46

tones. She couldn't hear what was being said, but she knew there was no hope. Slovie waited, but Benjamin didn't come back right away. When he did, Slovie asked him, "Who will take care of you and the children?"

Benjamin went to her and held her. There were tears and he told her, as he had so often, "Slovie, I love you."

Later Clara saw her father in the shop with his head in his hands, seated at the table, crying. The doctor had told Benjamin nothing could be done for Slovie. At first Benjamin didn't want to believe it. This couldn't happen to his family. Slovie was so young, and he needed her. He prayed and asked, *Why is this happening?* For a long time he wondered, *Why?* There had been no answers for him.

The summer with its heat ended, and fall came with all its wondrous colors.

One particularly lovely afternoon Slovie seemed better. Benjamin was beside himself with joy. She wanted to come sit at the window and see the outdoors. Clara had just finished brushing Slovie's hair, and she felt relaxed and looked better. Benjamin's heart leaped. *The doctor could be wrong,* he thought.

They helped her to the chair; she seemed happier as she drank in the beauty of the autumn. A light wind moved the fallen leaves along the ground.

"Open up the door; let in the breeze," she begged them.

Closing her eyes, she sat back and enjoyed the breeze as it played around her feet. There was a quiet serenity about her.

She sat forward. "Oh," she said, as if reminding herself, "we'll have nice weather for Rosh Hashanah." Everyone's spirits were lifted.

A few days later, Slovie died in her sleep. She was only twenty-six years old. She left a loving, close-knit family—a heartbroken husband, a shocked, saddened Clara, and Avram, too young to know. Clara was almost eight.

The day of the funeral was a mixed-up day, so many things happening. Neighbors came and took Avram. Clara wouldn't go. She sat on the bed and cried. The neighbors kept asking, "What will the children do? What will the children do?"

Clara remembered that night in her home. It looked strange. A *yarzeit* candle flickered on the table, the mirrors were covered, and neighbors came in and out. Avram was put to bed, a bewildered, tired little boy.

No one paid any attention to a forlorn Clara as she walked

around in the house, not knowing what to do, one little girl among so many adults. She went back and sat quietly in her favorite spot, on her mother's bed, looking at the floor. She didn't know what was going to happen next. Everything was different today: her mother wasn't here.

There were so many strangers and neighbors, Clara wished they would all go home. She fell asleep on her bed with her clothes on. When all had gone, Benjamin came in and covered her up. He didn't awaken her. Then he fell into bed. He buried his head in Slovie's pillow and sobbed.

His Slovie was gone!

Chapter 12
Life without Slovie

Benjamin, understandably, was a man consumed with grief at his wife's passing. He was strong. He was young. He had loved her and his little family. Their life was a struggle, but they had been happy. Whatever problems had come up, they were able to manage, to make it through. They had their faith, and they had each other.

At first, when Slovie became ill, Benjamin thought she would recover, that all she needed was rest. Families and friends had assured him of that. He had never imagined his life would, someday, go on without her. Now here he was, a widower with two young children to care for.

The children missed their mother. Benjamin often heard Clara sobbing at night. Mother and daughter had been close, a strong bond holding their lives together. Now an endearing link was gone. Benjamin's heart ached for his child. He was a good man, a good father, but he didn't know what to do to ease her loneliness. Clara was left alone to cope with the pain of her mother's death.

She kept busy with the chores and caring for Avram. When Clara was cooking, she would think of the conversations with her mother as she was learning to cook. At times this made her sad, when she realized how much she missed her mother. Other times Clara would remember something funny her mother had said, when they laughed together. A smile would half-break over her face and she felt a little better.

Sometimes Clara was angry at her mother for dying, for leaving her. Sometimes she questioned why it was her mother who had to die. She wondered what she had done that her mother had to die. Everyone else had a mother. Why not her? She cried and went off to the field where she had romped with her mother. The flowers that usually gladdened her heart and uplifted her spirits did nothing today. She walked around and around the field until she was so tired but never found answers to any of her questions here in her refuge.

At one point she wanted her mother to be there even if she had to remain in bed. Then finally Clara accepted it was better that her mother didn't have to suffer anymore.

The year for Benjamin was long days folded into longer nights, and then unfolding into long days again. He worked in the shop, but a thousand thoughts of Slovie raced through his head and it was difficult to keep his mind on work. He tried to keep a routine and have the children help him. He thought being busy was good for them. It helped a little, but the everyday life was full of a pain that didn't go away.

The matchmakers beat a path to Benjamin's door. It was too difficult for him to think of anyone in Slovie's place in his home. His grief, rooted deep inside him, enclosed him like a shell. For a while he could stave them off.

One matchmaker pointed out, correctly, the children's need for a woman to care for them. Another brought up a particular woman she had in mind for Benjamin. He remained noncommittal.

The winter came, with stinging cold and biting winds. Benjamin couldn't get enough wood to keep a constant fire in the stove. A revolt was on in the country, and he couldn't venture too far from the area to get wood. The house would warm up a little, but most of the time it was drafty and chilly. The children became ill and stayed in bed to keep warm. Benjamin cared for them as best he could, leaving them only to scrounge in the hills, collecting any wood he could find. Others in the little community were doing the same thing.

Benjamin piled the wood against one wall inside the house, instead of outdoors. When it snowed and the driving wind packed the snow down on the wood, it was difficult to separate quickly. It was always too cold to stay out for any length of time.

Benjamin, overworked, became ill, too. A neighbor found a woman who could come help the family. Hot soups and care soon had the children up and around. The woman told the children they could call her Tante (Aunt) Gittel.

Gittel was a petite woman, plain of face. She wore her hair primly back and rolled into a knot at the nape of her neck. A pleasant woman, she was soft-spoken. When she smiled, crinkles formed near the outer edges of her eyes.

Clara now helped care for Benjamin, so Gittel could help in the shop. The shop had been closed when Benjamin became ill. That had worried him. No money coming in would put him behind in paying the rent and providing food for the family. Gittel could help with some of the repairs.

When Benjamin was better, he reopened the shop full-time. He had always been a hard worker, ambitious, and knew a man, to be a man, must have work.

When the day's work was done and he entered the living quarters of the house, his nostrils were greeted with the wonderful familiar odors of cooking or baking Gittel was preparing. He could smile again, sometimes because he heard the laughter and chatter of his children once more. It was something that had been missing from his home.

Two difficult years had dragged on since Slovie's death. Slovie had worried about who would care for Benjamin and the children. Now, Benjamin thought he had the answer to Slovie's question. It wasn't with the matchmakers. Here in the house was the answer. Gittel!

Gittel! If she would have him, and the responsibility of the children. Taking care of them temporarily was one thing. Would she marry him and take on the task permanently?

It was Friday. Benjamin had been thinking of what he would say to Gittel that night after dinner. He had been thinking about it but kept putting it off. He didn't know what to do. Sometimes he thought it was right; then sometimes he wasn't so sure. He had loved Slovie. Could he be a good husband to Gittel? This troubled him deeply.

He thought of asking the rabbi, then decided against it. What could the rabbi know about Benjamin's feelings and his life? Besides, no one had a right to know anything about his personal life. It should be private, just between Gittel and himself.

The *Shabbos* table was set with candles and a small *challah* Gittel had baked. The children were happy, teasing and laughing. Gittel lighted the candles and said the *Shabbos* prayer. Then she served the meager dinner. The atmosphere was festive, so no one noticed how little food there was. Benjamin looked around the table. He hoped she would accept him so they could be a family again.

Benjamin walked Gittel home and finally got up the courage to discuss marriage with her. She had come to admire the man. He was a good and devoted father, greatly concerned for his children. He had been through much, yet never complained. He was honest and reliable and a good friend to many.

"I'll work hard, Gittel. I'll try to be a good husband to you." Benjamin looked at this woman he was asking to be his wife, share his home, and care for his children. He knew it would not be an easy life for her. He had put his hand ever so lightly on her shoulder and looked at her with a question in his eyes.

Gittel accepted. This would be her first marriage. She had been alone for a long time. It was a struggle for a woman to be alone. She made a meager living helping families (who didn't have much) when babies were born, when there was illness or death, wherever she was needed. While she was busy working her life went along and she didn't have time to feel the loneliness. It was when she returned home to her room that the emptiness of her life descended upon her, and she cried many times. Matchmakers never came to her. "Who would replace her in the much-needed work she does for the village?" they asked each other. Gittel didn't know that and was sure they ignored her because she was poor, with no dowry.

Gittel saw sickness and sadness in the homes she helped in, but they were families—together. The one thing she missed terribly was a family of her own. Now she would really belong to a family, Benjamin's family.

"I'll be a good wife to you and care for the children as if they were my own. They will be my own. Oh, Benjamin!" She was ecstatically happy. There were tears in her eyes. There were mutual benefits on both sides, and each was aware of the fact.

They were married. The new bride brought her few belongings, which included a small table, two chairs, a bed, some linens, and a few dishes. Clara would always remember the rug. It added so much to their home. The room looked better, and the floor was warmer because of it. The children enjoyed sitting on it in front of the stove. Clara now had her own bed. Gittel had given it to her. It was fixed with a pillow and nice, warm quilt. Clara felt grown-up. She was ten years old.

When Gittel came to stay at their home, it was difficult for Clara to accept her in Slovie's place. The girl couldn't understand her feelings, because she liked Gittel. But this child had loved her mother passionately and now felt she was betraying her mother's memory. Sometimes she felt angry and belligerent. It was something she couldn't comprehend.

Gittel was an understanding person. Patiently she accepted Clara's changing moods, always with a kind word. Gittel was there whenever the children needed her. Sometimes Clara's attitude worried Gittel, too. She wanted to be accepted. Eventually Clara's animosities disappeared. She came to love Gittel for the warm, caring person she was. Gittel worked hard to make this a truly loving family unit. The children still called her Tante Gittel, but she didn't mind. In her heart she knew they loved her.

Chapter 13
The Belascu Incident

The continued influx of Jewish immigrants into Romania became fertile ground for the growth of political anti-Semitism of the people, whose behavior was well learned by the pogroms in the Ukraine of Russia. Peasant revolts began to take place, exploding in 1903 with the most hideous outbursts of brutality against Jews. There were attacks on people on the streets and in the synagogues, desecration of cemeteries, burning of houses, and ransacking of businesses.

Every day brought new violence and new atrocities, many against young women. Jews now found it difficult to earn their livelihood. Landowners raised taxes and rents, and there were food shortages.

Benjamin and other Jews were alarmed at the reign of terror taking place near and around them. *Romania is becoming like Russia,* they worried.

They met in secret to discuss the problems. Some decided to leave for America. Others said they didn't have the money to go. They would have to wait and watch. *Things might change,* they hoped.

But in Benjamin old fears reawakened. He knew in his heart things wouldn't change. Someday soon his child Clara would have to leave for America. A shadow had fallen over them.

Then in 1907 another terrible revolt took place. In all Jewish hearts fear was constantly present. Clara was twelve.

A few years after the revolt, there were still killings and vicious beatings and hate harassment. Benjamin and his family lived in this hate-filled environment. With his family growing up, Benjamin was more anxious than ever to make a little more money. One way he could do this was to take his wares to the bazaar.

The bazaar was in the center of the village. It was divided into stalls, some larger than others. Everyone could go there once, but now very few stalls were rented to Jews. The peasants had protested that Jews were taking their livelihood. Still Benjamin decided to try it again. The fee for renting a stall was now doubled for a Jew. Benjamin waited in line. The guards kept pushing him back, letting others ahead of him. He was the last one to get a number for a stall.

When he found it, he was greatly disappointed. It was a very small space located at the very end of the bazaar. Very few people walked down to that section. Yet he was thankful to get one at all. He began setting out his wares.

He glanced out on the village square here in Vaslui. It was filled with bazaar stalls laden with wares of all kinds, dairy products of the districts, and fresh vegetables and fruits. Gaily colored clothes hung on lines, and handmade wares were displayed.

Already the square hummed with the sounds of the shopkeepers shouting their wares. Women in their shawls haggled with the shopkeepers, and then there were the laughter and other noises of children.

Benjamin puzzled over his good fortune in obtaining the stall. His spirits lifted and he was optimistic, because the square was busy at the other end. He had hopes that some would wander down to his end of the bazaar.

Benjamin's wares were different from the others'. Cutting and hand-sewing small fur pelts into coat collars and hats was a trade he had learned. Here in Romania it was almost impossible to buy the fur he needed. It was priced beyond what he could afford. Many times he bartered his skillful repairs of fur coats and capes for the wealthy in order to obtain an extra pelt or piece of fur. When he had enough pieces, he created wonderful fur caps and fur collars. Out of sheepskins he made men's vests.

On this day Benjamin set up a few wooden stands he had made and displayed his precious caps and fur collars, pieces for the approaching winter. Benjamin stood outside the stall waiting, hoping someone would have need of his merchandise.

"Rothman! Rothman! Push back your stands. Back!" the angry guttural voice of the soldier Belascu thundered at Benjamin. Belascu, dressed in the uniform of the hated Black Guard of the Romanian army, rode forward, a most menacing figure. He was a giant of a man, like all those privileged to serve in the elite Black Guard. Up he rode into the stall, and drawing his sword, he pushed it tightly against Benjamin' chest and pinned him against the wall of the stall.

Then quickly, deftly, Belascu drew the sword upward, pushing its cold tip under Benjamin's chin on his windpipe. Holding it there, the soldier began to laugh, knowing full well any move the victim made would result in a cut throat. Benjamin stood there, angry and frightened at the same time.

Finally Belascu withdrew the sword and rode back to some of

the troops standing watch outside the square. All were laughing uproariously. Belascu was loyal to the Romanian government. He obeyed his orders, which were to keep watch over the people. His special orders were to keep Jews under strictest surveillance, and his harassment of them was constant.

Benjamin began to pick up a few of the stands that had fallen and was nearly finished when Belascu came riding back fast and furious. His horse's hooves clanging on the cobblestones echoed resoundingly through the square. The soldier knocked the wares to the ground, cutting some of the fur pieces. Benjamin barely had time to run to a corner of the stall. He hit the cement wall so hard, he scratched and bruised his arm and back. The sword knocked Benjamin's cap off; then Belascu rode off again with the cap sitting on the tip of his upraised sword.

The other shopkeepers, in sympathy with the government against Jews, raised their angry voices. "Go home, Jew! Go home, Jew!" they taunted Benjamin. No one came to help him set up his stall again.

Benjamin now understood how he had had the "good fortune" to get a stall today. Belascu had managed it, having chosen Benjamin as the privileged recipient of his devilish treatment for the day. Belascu chose one Jew a week for his vicious attacks of harassment.

Benjamin knew no matter how many times he set up his wares, Belascu would strike them down. Quietly he began to pack his things. He was frustrated and frightened, and again anger filled his being. He had paid a fee for the stall, a doubled fee, and he had sold nothing. He salvaged a few pieces that had not been cut and gathered up the odd pieces of fur.

On his way home he decided to stop and try to sell something. He did manage to sell a few pieces. He was thankful. It was the little extra he needed to earn. The rest of the way home he went over the incident with Belascu. It reminded him of Russia. The happenings of anti-Semitism were occurring too frequently for him not to pay attention.

Benjamin worried not for himself, but for his family, especially Clara, a young girl. He knew he had to save so Clara could leave Romania—not to go to another country in Europe, for he saw anti-Semitism everywhere there, but to go to America. She would go. He would see to that!

55

Chapter 14

Clara and Friends

Rochel Leah and Shlomo Solomon were neighbors of the Rothmans who lived around the corner. Their children, Liz and Usher, became close friends with Clara. Liz was one year older than Clara, and Usher was three years older. The threesome went everywhere together.

There was very little money to spend, so the group's entertainment was limited. This didn't stop them from having fun and enjoying themselves. In summer the fields and meadows were thick carpets of flowers that Clara and her friends raced through. The sun was hot and the skies cloudless as the children walked along streams and stopped to enjoy a bit of lunch or fruit.

There were long walks home with laughter and talking. They all had dreams, and there was the enjoyment of the innocence of their time. They always had fun, whatever they did, but the times they enjoyed most were the festivals.

Romania was long regarded as the breadbasket of Europe because of its long growing season and abundant harvests. There was always a festival for young and old. People from all regions would attend.

The grapevines had been heavily laden with fruit. The harvest had been exceptionally abundant. The government and landowners were pleased and happy. There would be a celebration with the grape festival. Clara and her friends had made plans to go. It was an opportunity to be away from the restricted area for a short time.

Everyone would be dressed in the folk costumes of their regions. The costumes varied a little from region to region. This was a special night for Clara. Gittel had promised to make her a new dress. All week she worked on it, and Clara did her share, helping with other chores at home. When the dress was finished, Clara, as any young girl would be, was anxious to wear it. It was so beautiful. She kept touching it over and over.

It had a blouse of lovely sheer white cotton with full puffed sleeves and ruffles at the wrists. Around the neck and down the sleeves it was embroidered with beautiful flowers of all colors. Young girls in this area from early on were taught by mothers how to do the intricate embroidery. They all became expert at it. Red strings drew the neckline closed and tied into a tasseled bow.

There was an apron skirt of dark cotton with a bib top and straps criss-crossing in the back, buttoned at the waist. Embroidered bands of the rainbow-colored flowers ran down the sides of the apron and across the bottom. This was worn over a full white underskirt. Clara had helped with the embroidery so it would be ready in time. Although there would be many similar to it from the region, Clara felt hers was special. Clara was growing up!

The day of the festival finally arrived. Liz and Clara braided each other's long hair with ribbons and flowers, as was the custom for unmarried women. Later Liz and Usher came back for Clara. They set off, all in a festive mood. When they got to the village, there were hundreds of bright-glowing candles and people laughing and singing and so much food, everywhere they looked.

People were dancing the Romanian national dance, the hora, done in a circle. The three waited and when there was a break in the chain, Usher rushed in, pulling the girls with him, and they joined in the dance. Their happy faces were flushed with excitement, and the lighted candles cast reflections in their shining eyes. Usher held onto Clara's hand as they danced to the wonderful music of the night. They were so happy, youth having its fling!

All too soon it was ending for them. They didn't want to leave but had to get back to their restricted areas to avoid trouble. On the way home they passed a Gypsy encampment, a caravan of wagons. They were there that night but would be gone in the morning—harassed by the officials and forced to move on. There were camp fires near some of the tents. Clara and the others stopped by the roadside and watched. Other festival goers walked among the tents, where children begged for money. Dark-eyed, scantily dressed girls danced, then held out their tambourines for money. Gypsy musicians played their dulcimers and violins. The hauntingly plaintive music filled the air and brought longing to those who heard it.

Outside one tent, people were standing in line to have their fortunes told. Liz, Usher, and Clara took their places in line. The girls wanted their fortunes told. Clara went in first. An older Gypsy woman sat at a small table covered with a dirty cloth. A lamp hanging on a nail threw a dim yellowish light around the darkened tent.

The Gypsy woman was preoccupied with shuffling the cards; then she motioned Clara to come sit at the table. The woman, with business in mind, first held out her hand for money. Then accepting the coin Clara put there, she proceeded to "throw the cards," as she put it.

Carefully the woman pulled a card from the deck, looked at it, nodded as if she approved, then put it down in front of her on the table. Clara watched, fascinated, as the woman pulled cards and set them down side by side. Sometimes she grunted and shook her head no, then at different times she nodded her head yes. Then she counted the cards, touching different ones, straightening them. She drew her brows together and shook her head. Then she told Clara what every young girl wants to hear about: love! Pointing to a card, she said, "There is one in love with you, but he will go far away."

Clara watched as the woman touched other cards, saying, "You will cross many waters, and there are many tears in your life."

The Gypsy then put the cards together and motioned that she was finished.

Usher was next but wouldn't go in. He thought it was all foolishness. Liz took her turn. The Gypsy told her, too, "You will cross a large water."

When Liz came out, Usher was sure he was right. "She tells the same story to everybody," he said.

Clara and Liz laughed at their fortunes. "She's meshuga [crazy]." They would never leave home, family, and friends. It was unthinkable! They walked home talking excitedly about the wonderful time they'd had.

Usher was in the middle, with Liz and Clara on either side of him. Clara looked up at the clear, dark sky twinkling with millions of stars. Her heart was light. Usher was holding her hand. They were young and for the moment forgot their restricted lives, forgot the poverty and the misery it brought. For the moment, life held promise of better things. This was youth dreaming and impatient for these dreams to be fulfilled.

Chapter 15

The Solomons Leave

While Clara and her friends were growing up, the world around them became more chaotic. Each day brought disturbing news of some new trouble in their area. In neighboring cities there were pogroms. The many incidents couldn't be ignored. Jewish parents became anxious to get their children away. Facing these separations brought torment to these parents' souls, but they knew flight was the only means to survival.

All these parents had a dream to see their children in America. To many, it was an impossible dream. It would take money, and many were too poor, with no hope of ever obtaining the needed funds. Everyone had heard of the many wonders in America. They discussed it in disbelief.

"People can go anywhere. There are no soldiers to stop them. How can that be?" they asked each other.

Others discussed the matter of work. They had heard there was work for everyone in America. It didn't matter if one was a Jew. Whatever a person earned belonged to him. In awed wonder, they spoke of these miracles in the "Golden Land," America!

Clara and Liz, in their early teens, were very close friends. Liz came over to talk to her friend. Problems were easier to bear when there was a friend to share them with.

Liz's parents had gotten permission for Usher to go to America. Liz couldn't hold back the tears.

"We argue and disagree on many things. They all seem so unimportant now." Liz was worried. Her brother was going so far away, and she couldn't accept that.

Clara, listening to her friend pouring out her young heart, felt the tears brimming in her eyes, too. She wiped them away in anger. *Why?* she wondered. Even though there were problems in the government, why couldn't the Jews be allowed to live their lives in peace with their families? She couldn't understand.

It had taken money to get Usher the passport and necessary papers. In Romania he didn't have a job. He *couldn't* get work, as it was becoming increasingly difficult for a Jew to work here. In America he would be helped. A Jewish organization would see that he learned a trade. He would have a job. He would at least have a chance.

When Usher was ready to leave, Clara came to say good-bye. It was difficult to part with a friend who was embarking on so long a voyage, to a country far away. She was sure she would never see him again.

Usher knew he would miss Clara. He wished he didn't have to go because of the resurgence of anti-Semitic uprisings. His feelings for his family were deep-rooted. He loved them. He wondered what it would be like to be so far from them. He was leaving with a hope that he would be able to make enough money in America to send for his parents and sister. It would take time, but he would work toward that end. The year was 1908.

After Usher left, Liz and Clara spent time together, but not as often as before. Liz was preparing to go to America. Her parents were trying to get her a passport.

Mail came from Usher. The letters postmarked "U.S.A." made them so proud! Usher had been the first from their area to go to America. The letters told of his trip over in the ship. He had come steerage class. The trip had been long, and he had been ill. He had landed at Ellis Island.

There were so many Jews coming from Eastern Europe to America that the Department of Immigration was seriously considering limiting the number of Jews coming in. After much debating and the intercession of Jewish organizations with the government, their entrance here would continue, but the Jewish organizations had given their word that Jews coming in would have jobs and be self-sufficient and no burden to the government.

Usher was detained on Ellis Island and then released to an organization in New York City. The organization made arrangements for him to get a room, shared with another boarder. Some Jewish families who had come to New York couldn't earn enough for their families, so they supplemented their income by renting out rooms. Two boarders, staying in a small room, helped pay rent and food.

Usher and the other boarders received two meals a day. Their breakfast wasn't much—bread or rolls, often stale, and coffee or tea. Dinner was a little more substantial, depending on who the lady of the house was. The more fortunate boarders were those staying in homes of women who were warmhearted good cooks! Second helpings were usually proffered there.

Usher was apprenticed to a baker and worked hard in a small bakery shop. His room and board were paid for by the organization until he earned his own money. As soon as he learned the job well, he would be moved out to another state.

The organization was overworked in an effort to get the immigrants out of New York as quickly as possible. In some letters, Usher praised the organizations helping him. "It can only happen in America," he wrote.

Usher's letters complained about the work: "It is hard to get up at three or four o'clock in the morning to get the bread ready." His constant lament was that he missed everybody. He was living with strangers. Every day strangers! Everywhere strangers!

He was finally moved out of New York and sent on the train to Minneapolis, Minnesota. There he had a job waiting for him. It was in a bakery on the north side of town, in an area populated mostly with Jews. His letters sounded happier now.

In his letters, Usher constantly expounded the positive now. America was wonderful. Everything they had heard about it was true. There were no soldiers on the streets. No one bothered him. He was free to go anywhere by himself. He wasn't afraid. He could go to the synagogue. Stores closed early on Friday and were closed on the Sabbath. He had one room for himself. He worked and was paid and could keep his money. With pride he wrote: "I am saving to send Liz her ticket."

He always sent regards to Clara.

The next year Liz received her ticket. Usher was anxiously waiting for her to come. Liz didn't have any problem coming to America, as she had a sponsor, her brother, who would help her get started.

A few weeks later Liz left Vaslui, leaving a saddened, lonely Clara. An optimist, Clara usually saw the bright side of things. However, when some events came to pass the bright side was obscured, a bit more difficult to discern, and so it was when Liz had gone. Clara was sure she would never see her friend again.

It seemed Clara's life was constantly being interrupted, constantly changing. Nothing was permanent. Still, she was a young lady growing up. She wondered what other changes there would be. What would she do now with Usher and Liz both gone?

The year was 1910. Clara was fifteen years old.

Part II

The Golden Land

Chapter 16

The Decision

There were endless days and sleepless nights for young Clara after Liz had gone. They had spent much time together, and as in all things in the everyday life of the young, the friendship had been taken for granted. They thought it would always be there. Changes were never contemplated, and life for them had gone along with a day-to-day permanence.

Now, as the days passed, Clara felt the absence of her friend more keenly. Things to do around the house and other attempts at keeping busy failed miserably.

She walked the fields where both had gone to talk and dream but found little solace there. She came home even more restless and then again, was drawn to the outdoors where she sometimes sat in the fields for hours, quietly unhappy, her thoughts roaming far away to wherever Liz was.

Gently Gittel tried to persuade Clara to busy herself with something, like sewing. Gittel at one time had been fortunate enough to have been apprenticed to a very fine staff who did dressmaking and mending for a few of the wealthy families of the city. She now wanted to teach Clara the art of these fine techniques.

"What do I need to learn that for?" Clara would argue. "I'll never use it here."

"Maybe not, but it doesn't hurt to learn how to do anything. Whatever you learn you keep! No one can ever take that away from you." They argued back and forth and couldn't seem to resolve the problem.

Fabrics, like all commodities, were very hard to come by because of shortages and little or no money. Gittel remedied this situation by ripping up a pair of worn-out pants. She showed Clara how to make a skirt out of them. The girl learned to finish the item with tiny stitches and fine detail so it looked professional and stylish.

Clara became very interested in the challenges this sewing experience presented to her. Out of old things she learned to create new things, making up her own designs and patterns—the possibilities were endless. She was very creative and even surprised Gittel with her ingenuity. All in all, Clara derived much satisfaction from this newfound ability of hers.

Gittel, in relating Clara's accomplishments to Benjamin, was most ecstatic. "She has such a good head on her shoulders. I show her once, and she knows how to do it. It's remarkable." Gittel spoke with a mother's pride in her voice.

And Clara had found a way to keep busy while she waited for word from her friends.

Usher sent letters through American organizations helping the immigrants in America. Many times letters came that clearly showed they had been tampered with; letters were delayed and delivered months later. Letters from America often originally contained money to help the family left behind. The letters were intercepted at various points, the money taken, and the letters destroyed. There were never any reasons or explanations given to those eagerly waiting for mail that never came.

No matter! Whenever a letter did come, Clara was overjoyed to hear from her friends. Anxious to know how they were faring in America, she hung on every word, and the letters were read and reread over and over again, as if there would be something new to hear or something had been missed in one of the readings.

Life was a struggle at this time for Clara and her family in Romania. Clara was resigned to staying with her parents and couldn't ever imagine leaving them.

The Solomons had been gone almost two years. Life went on in the village, with old worries and the new economic and political worries!

In 1912, Bulgaria, Serbia, and Greece declared war on Turkey. It was the first Balkan war. The Bulgarians fought and won many campaigns, acquiring new territories. This infuriated Romania, which then sought from the Western world the restoration of a piece of southern Bulgaria known as Dobruja, a province between Romania and Bulgaria on the Black Sea.

Romania clamored for war with Bulgaria. Food supplies, already short, were now taken from the people and given to the army, causing severe food shortages, which led to starvation in many areas.

Romania's barbaric brutalization of Jews became worse in the country, as Jews were blamed for the situation. Outbreaks of riots began again.

Once more Benjamin and Gittel became greatly concerned for

Clara's safety from the angry peasant neighbors and soldiers. Young, pretty girls, especially Jewish ones, were the target for kidnap and rape.

The parents were forced, once again, to think of America for Clara. One thing they knew for certain—she would have no trouble entering the country, as she could support herself by sewing. She had become quite adept at it. This was a very important requisite for the Department of Immigration of the United States.

Benjamin, remembering his own journey with its perils and fears, worried about a girl going to America alone. He tried to console himself on sleepless nights that his daughter would be free in the Golden Land. She would be free of the anti-Semitism that was always here. It was a strong, hateful undercurrent they had to deal with in their daily lives.

The hate was everywhere and getting worse. Nothing was done to curb it. Instead, perpetrators were charged to do more harm to Jews, with more beatings and killings!

It was almost impossible for Benjamin to make a living. He couldn't go to the bazaar anymore to sell any of his merchandise. It was forbidden for Jews. The situation was becoming more unbearable with each passing day.

First and foremost in Benjamin's mind was getting his daughter away. He began making the arrangements for her to leave and the government didn't make it easy with their questions and delays.

This was a time of soul-searching for Benjamin. As bad as the situation was, he wondered, *Am I doing the right thing sending her away? And is this the appropriate time or should I wait?*

He didn't know.

There was much self-doubt and worry. He thought of other parents, in past generations, and many now who faced the same dilemma. They all had to make the decision to let their children go or stay. To save them, there was only one decision that could be made. Benjamin knew that. Deep in his troubled mind, he knew that. It was a time to be strong of heart in spite of his many misgivings. He prayed to make the right decision. He would help her get away!

Once the decision had been made, the parents hastened to ready Clara for departure.

"At least one nice outfit for the trip to America," Gittel told Benjamin as she began sewing, making over her clothes for Clara. Gittel would miss this child of hers, a child not of her flesh and blood, but of her heart. For days she had put out of her mind how life would be without Clara here. She told herself, *It is best for Clara,* but the gnawing fear didn't disappear.

Telling Clara they had decided she must leave was another difficult task for the parents. How do you tell your child you are sending her away? The parents found the right words. They told her she was going to America, where she would have a better life and be free.

True, the circumstances around them were life-threatening, but she didn't want to leave her family. It was difficult for her to understand. She loved them, and America was so far away.

"And what about you?" she cried.

She had seen how lonesome Liz's parents were and had visited them when she could. If she went away, there would be no one for them, or her parents.

The discussion went on for a few days more. Finally, Clara knew she would listen to her parents. They knew best. They wanted a better life for her and were sacrificing much for her to be free.

Benjamin had scrounged, saved, and done without. He had saved bit by little bit for an emergency. Always he hoped it wouldn't come, but the fear that it could had lived within him for a long while. Now it was here!

Benjamin, after much harassment and numerous unnecessary trips back and forth to the authorities, finally got the railway and steamship tickets. That night he proudly held them up, saying, "This will be good for my *kynd* [child]."

He had mixed feelings. When he thought of her leaving, he was inconsolably saddened. When he remembered why she was going—to save herself, to be free—he was greatly heartened!

Benjamin had inquired wherever he could about the route Clara would be taking. Patiently, while his heart ached for her, he outlined it to her. He told her she would go through many countries, then to Berlin, Germany, and on to the Netherlands (Holland) and to Rotterdam. There she would get on a big ship. He told her, "People say it's a big ship."

While fears and anxieties ran rampant in his brain, Benjamin answered as many of Clara's questions as he could to allay her fears.

"You'll be all right. There are people, our people, at train stops who will help you." Benjamin put his arms around his daughter and held her. He could feel her trembling.

Benjamin always put his faith in God. That night, as he would many nights, he prayed, *God go with her. God go with her.*

At night Gittel tried to stifle her sobs in her pillow. Benjamin let her cry. In his mind he was going over all that he wanted to stress to his daughter: not to worry, to be careful, to write, to take care of herself, etc. The list went on and on, the concerns of a loving father.

He wished he had more to give her, but it had taken everything he had to get her passport and tickets.

He had many worries that he didn't voice. He thought about where she was going. He had made it possible for her to go to America, with a good chance for a better life than she would have in Romania. She would be free!

He had worried and fretted for months; now—with that last thought of her, free in America—Benjamin knew he had made the right decision. He tossed and turned for a long while, finally falling into a semifitful sleep.

Chapter 17

On Her Way

Clara left Vaslui the first week in March 1912. Her father's heart was heavy-laden as he drove the family to the station in his old horse-drawn cart. He had trouble guiding the horse and thus was spared the anguish of entering into any coversation.

"Where did you put the money?" Gittel inquired.

"In here." Clara pointed to the inside of her blouse, where she had been told to put it. It was the third time Gittel had raised the question, but Clara understood. She had only to look at Gittel and see the pain in her eyes, pain that couldn't be masked by attempts at conversation.

They had talked much the night before, but there was still more each wanted to say. Why is it sometimes difficult to speak what is really in the heart, to express true feelings? Why are they concealed, waiting for another time—a time that may not come? So it was now. They were all in various stages of anxiety. Sometimes they were all quiet except for the clicking sounds Benjamin made while he nudged the horse forward. Other times Clara, Gittel, and Avram caught themselves all chattering together, the conversation tapering off until they were all silent—but their silence spoke volumes.

When they arrived at the station, Clara was surprised at the different things she saw there. She watched a troop train readying to leave. Young women and older women, perhaps wives and sweethearts, were saying their farewells. Soldiers were there being embraced with love and tears. It had never occurred to Clara that soldiers had loved ones or could love, since she knew them only as ruthless killers. They were soldiers in an army that persecuted and oppressed her people. She turned her head away, not wanting to see any more.

The family waited for a long time before Clara's train came rattling in on one of the other tracks. The noise at the station had become deafening, with train wheels clanging, whistles blowing, and the sounds of the crowd adding to the din. The family huddled together to hear each other talk.

When it was time to board, the good-byes with Clara's parents were long and tearful. Clara thought, *If only we could all go together.*

Then she hugged them again and again ever so tightly; it was hard to let go.

Avram clung to her skirt while he sobbed uncontrollably. He was too young to understand it all. He only knew his Clara was going far away. His young mind didn't even know what "far away" meant.

She knelt and kissed his wet cheeks as she straightened his cap. She hugged him, feeling the warmth of his little body against hers. That little face smudged with his tears became a picture indelibly printed on her mind, and she would recall the moment many times.

Tearfully Clara made it up the steps and glanced back at her little family standing there. She realized the enormity of what was happening—her family was being broken up.

Clara made her way through the train and watched her family running along outside. She found her seat and waved at them. For a moment she had a wild urge to pick up her bags and run out to them, they looked so forlorn.

As she settled down, she caught a glimpse of her reflection in the train window. With her hat on, she looked so grown-up. Her parents saw this, too, but they worried, *Is she grown-up enough to go out into the world alone?*

Clara searched the crowd for her family and caught sight of them. She waved again as the train started moving out, swaying from side to side as it picked up speed, then rolled along the tracks unwinding before it, and Clara was on her way!

The train stopped at many places, and Clara saw crowds of people milling about outside. She saw a different part of life she was not used to. She was awestruck at women in beautiful clothes and men who looked prosperous and well fed. She had never seen these sights even near the settlement where she lived. She thought of the cruel winter that had just passed—how people had suffered and were wearing threadbare clothing. Everyone was so thin, as there had been severe food shortages, and many had starved. This was a different world outside the ghetto! She couldn't understand the contradiction—or comprehend the world that let non-Jews have much and Jews have little or nothing. Why the punishment of Jews? All she knew was how sad it made her. No one seemed to have the answer, so how could she?

The many days on the train were tiring, though at first it was exciting to see the different people in the towns. Clara envied them. They could remain in their homes, safe and secure. She wondered again who they were to have these privileges. She knew they weren't Jews.

Other times, just looking out the window became boring. There was so much of a sameness as towns and countryside rushed by.

The travelers ate out of bags and boxes and suitcases. Clara had black bread spread with cherry preserves made from cherries from their tree. Clara loved the preserves. They brought happy memories to her, of climbing the cherry tree and picking the cherries, wonderful thoughts of home that made her smile.

There was much going on in some of the different countries. Oppressed peasants, enemies of the nobles of the state, were rebelling. This was a constant state of affairs. Groups were dangerously unruly, and sometimes when the train stopped they could be seen roaming around the towns. They carried sticks and clubs and were noisy and angry, looking to start trouble somewhere, anywhere. There were times when they hurled stones and rocks at the train windows. The passengers were frightened and hid on the floor until the train got safely away.

The trip was mostly by train. Some countries Clara crossed were in disarray and much confusion. Europe was on the verge of World War I. Some countries were already embattled. People could see trouble was coming, and those who could were trying to leave.

The train traveled northward, and whenever it stopped now Clara saw the crowds of men, women, and children waiting. Clara saw the terror in their faces. It was somethng she had seen many times before, and it frightened her. There was prewar hysteria everywhere.

Clara watched people as they clawed their way over each other trying to get on the already crowded train to get away—anywhere! The conductor had difficulty keeping them away from the gates. Many were there with what little they could carry. They had waited for days in the cold, in the rain, hoping to get on. It had been their only hope, their only way to safety, and they were denied passage. They became angry, shouting and crying, and then fighting among them broke out. It was horrible to watch, and Clara felt helpless. If only there was something she could do. A person wants to help, and it's frustrating to look at the misery and have to turn away.

Clara sat down and listened to the other passengers, some sympathetic and others not. She was on her way, escaping from all this—but she thought of her parents, and couldn't help but worry about the uncertainty for them. She fell asleep fearing for her family and awoke later, frightened by nightmares she had about soldiers fighting near her home.

Clara's journey took her to Budapest, Hungary, where she saw beautiful buildings, wonderful land, and the people. Her thoughts went to Liz. Clara wondered if her friend had seen all the things she had seen. Was it possible Liz had come the same way, or had traveled another route? They would have all this to discuss and much more. Clara missed her friends. When would she see them? And when she did, would they be happy to see her?

Another thing that worried her: She had come so far, how much longer would her trip take? When would it end? In an optimistic mood, she answered herself, *Soon. I know it will be soon!*

At one point Clara and some of the passengers caught a boat that took them up the Danube. This was a totally new experience for her.

It wasn't a very large boat, and Clara could see others like it traveling up and down the river. She was curious. Where were they all going, and who were they? Were there others like herself being sent away?

Clara caught another train after leaving the boat. After an uneventful ride, they stopped at Vienna. It looked so beautiful, but later Clara heard of the devastating anti-Semitism of the Austrians. She would always think of how the beauty of the land, for her, was marred forever because of the evil there!

During the day she could see fields and forests and sometimes people. At night she looked out into darkness, seeing the lights of streets and in homes as the whistle blew and the train rolled on. She got used to the clanking noise of the train wheels, so loud at times it hurt her head. At night the constancy of it lulled her to sleep.

In Germany they were held up at a junction, then moved on to Berlin. Clara was to change trains here. It was a huge station where a multitude of passengers gathered as they left the different trains. Everyone seemed to know where he was going except Clara. People were being met by others. She felt homesick as she watched one family embracing.

Clara could feel a tear and wiped it away. She didn't want to cry, but sometimes it was extremely difficult not to, when she thought of home and how far from her family she had come. The worst was nurturing the thought that she would see them someday, knowing full well the improbability of that wish being fulfilled.

Time was passing and she was becoming uneasy waiting at this huge place. Many of the other passengers had gone, and she stood there alone on the platform, anxious for her train's arrival.

She went up to the station master and showed him her papers. He looked at them and said, "Rotterdam." She smiled and nodded her head. He knew which train she was to take.

It arrived and she was helped up the steps into the car and found a seat. This train was not full, which was unusual. Quickly she set her boxes down and settled in, nervous but relieved that she was on the right train.

When the train started she was on the last lap of her journey, which would take her to Holland.

At Rotterdam Clara was amazed at the huge port. It sprawled out with its shipyards, freighters from many lands tied to the wharves. There were big ships, like her father had told her. There were small boats and sailboats, too. Clara could never have imagined a place like this. Some ships were larger than many villages.

Holland was the best place of all the places she had been to—perhaps because it was the last country she had to cross before going to America.

She noticed another thing—the people didn't look fearful; their faces were happier than those she had seen in other countries.

It was a beautiful place, with quiet canals and spring flower–banked roads. So rapt was she in the scenic beauty around her, she had not planned on her next experience.

She headed in the wrong direction for her pier. Not realizing it, she walked an indeterminate length of time before she became aware of her error.

Anxious and frightened, she approached the only people she saw, two men working off the road. They had observed the young woman clutching her few belongings and knew her predicament. They were accustomed to people from different lands coming here to board ships, then becoming confused and losing their way.

The men were very sympathetic as Clara showed them her steamship ticket. Her fright dissipated a bit, as in kind tones they pointed her in the right direction to her pier. It was a long way off. She was told to hurry.

The weight of her few belongings became cumbersome, perhaps

because she was very tired. The long walk back took precious time she couldn't spare. She had to make it back.

What if the ship goes without me? What will I do here in a strange land? These were distinct possibilities if she couldn't make it back in time. She began to run but had to stop for a while to catch her breath. The distances between the piers were long, and she wondered, *Will I make it?*

Clara had come this far and an error could keep her from catching her boat. *That won't happen. I can't let it happen.*

Every instinct propelled her forward, and on Clara ran to where she could see people gathering.

Chapter 18

Across Many Waters

With a final spurt of energy, Clara raced to the pier where her ship was docked. She stopped and rested against a wire fence, as people were waiting impatiently to go up the plank onto the ship, a huge ship that seemed to reach into the sky with its tall smokestacks.

Clara took her place in the line, which was moving along at a snail's pace. In her hand she clutched her passport and tickets.

There were loud noises here, not concentrated in one spot, but coming from different areas. Shrill ships' whistles pierced the air, mingling with some that sounded like foghorns. Over all could be heard the voices of hundreds of people—passengers and workmen—shouting, some laughing, calling to each other in their different languages.

On board ship, when Clara finally got there, an officer checked her papers and motioned her to some stairs leading downward to the decks below. Men, women, and children, carrying bundles, talking excitedly, and gesticulating wildly, carefully made their way down the stairs. There was a great clatter as their feet tromped heavily, wearily, on the metal steps. Children trying to come up the stairs pushed and jostled the tired passengers coming down. Some became angry and shouted in their different tongues. The noise and excitement were touching everyone in one way or another.

The stairs were very crowded and Clara, making her way down, was being pushed from behind. She could not see the steps and almost fell over a woman and child in front of her.

When she made it down to the two decks below, steerage class, where the poor passengers were, she couldn't believe the sights there. There were hundreds of people in this crowded part of the ship. They were stretched out on the floor, sleeping on some of their belongings. Many sat huddled on bags and bundles. There were many crying children of all ages, from infants on up. Mothers, looking worn and tired, were trying to feed some. It was bedlam!

The trip took almost two weeks. Frequent storms on the Atlantic pummeled the huge ship, and it creaked and groaned as the frightened passengers huddled together, sure the ship would break in half—some cried, while religious ones prayed.

Clara and the other passengers became deathly ill, some with infections, others with colds, running high fevers, or pneumonia. Almost everyone became seasick and vomited wherever they had to. The air was foul and stale, and it was so cold and damp Clara's bones ached.

Something nice and hot to eat or drink would have been well appreciated. She could only think about it—and imagine sipping hot soup. She closed her eyes and felt warmer.

When she recuperated, she came up on deck for a breath of fresh air. "It won't be long now," she whispered to herself. "It can't be too much longer!"

One day on deck Clara heard excited voices and cries: "There it is! There it is!"

People came running to both sides of the ship. Clara didn't know what the excitement was about. It was foggy, but then she could see tops of trees and land. Then out of the fog and mist she saw it: the Statue of Liberty. What a wondrous sight, beckoning the immigrants to come, to taste freedom! It gave Clara goose bumps. People knelt on deck and prayed. Ships were passing in all directions. Those on board waved greetings. The fog began to clear, and Clara saw America!

Clara could not believe she was finally here. The trip had been a long, arduous one. Parted from those she loved, she had come on this journey, crossing into many lands alone and crossing many waters. With that thought came another—she remembered going to the Gypsy camp with Usher and Liz and hearing: "You will cross many waters." Usher had pooh-poohed it. Still, here she was in America after crossing "many waters." What did she make of it? She couldn't say. She had many mixed emotions about being here. She had arrived where her parents believed it was best for her to be. They had sacrificed much, but the worst was the cutoff from family. She had come through it suffering illness, a wretched trip across in the bowels of the ship, and alone. How proud her parents would be when she wrote them—she was here in America!

The ship docked in New York harbor on April 15, 1912. Small ferries came out to the ship and brought Clara and others to Ellis Island. It was a huge place and filled the newcomers with dread and anxiety! They were pushed and shoved and herded into a large room with benches. People with their meager bundles of belongings were sleeping on the floor or benches. The air was filled with deafening noises. There were no empty benches. A very tired Clara looked around, then walked to a wall, set her boxes on the floor, and sat on them. She was cold and hungry but filled with an excitement that outweighed any discomfort she felt.

At Ellis Island they had what was known as a "few seconds medical exam." Doctors checked for disease as newcomers came by in endless lines. If there was any doubt about a disease, an immigrant's shoulder was marked with chalk. This meant delay and further examination, causing the unfortunate ones worry that they might be deported. They cried and prayed and waited. They waited again in long lines to see other doctors, doctors who were abrupt and without compassion because they were overworked and tired.

Immigrants who were not detained because of disease went through the examination in about five hours.

Clara was nervous as she went into the room. She had some very anxious moments until a Yiddish interpreter appeared and helped Clara get through the paperwork. Then she had to wait again until the interpreter came back and explained that Clara was all right and could continue on with the rest of the examination. At her next stop she was questioned about her ability to work.

Hatred of Jews in the world brought about a constant stream of immigrants pouring into the United States, year by year. This alarmed American leaders. Their concern was that the high standard of living synonymous with American work would be brought down by the competition of cheap labor.

At the opening of the twentieth century, attempts were made to reduce the number of immigrants. Congress wanted literacy tests and some form of certification of character from the home country. This would have cut off Jewish immigration from Russia and Romania, as Jews could not get certification from these countries, so full of brutal bigotry. Passing literacy tests was impossible, since schooling for Jews had been prohibited for such a long time. President Taft vetoed these requirements when it passed through a new congress.

Clara was fortunate to enter America after these requirements were defeated. She told the interpreter, "I am a good seamstress." She came, at age seventeen, with only her sewing skills, a few boxes, and very little money.

At Ellis Island Clara was sent to another line where she got a tag pinned on her that specified her railway destination. Hers was the state of Minnesota. She was going to Minneapolis, Minnesota, where Usher and Liz were.

Clara was given food, including an orange. She was quite

famished and ate it all quickly. It tasted good, and the orange refreshed her. She and other immigrants were taken by boat across to New York to the train station. She heard the announcement in Yiddish come over the loudspeaker that her train was in and would leave soon. A guide helped Clara find the right gate to the track. She boarded the train for the last leg of her journey. Soon it was snaking its way over a maze of tracks and out of the New York station, heading westward.

Clara was worn out from the ordeal of long lines, examinations, and the hundreds of questions asked by the interpreters. She could no longer fight the exhaustion and fell asleep. The next day the train crossed New York to Pennsylvania and then rolled through Cleveland, Ohio.

Clara had been extremely careful of the money she had with her. She spent very little, managing as best she could, sometimes going hungry. She was fearful of arriving in America with most of her money gone.

Now, almost at her destination, Clara felt she could spend a little. She saw other passengers stop the man carrying a tray of food products. They gave him money and then took something. Clara watched their looks of pleasure as they chewed.

Clara stopped the man and looked at the products. There were only a few, and she chose one. Then she held her hand out with some coins in it. The man took one and left. Clara peeled the paper off and took a bite of chocolate. She chewed it, then kept it in her mouth as it melted and slowly trickled down her throat. She made it last as long as she could. It tasted heavenly.

At Chicago, Illinois, Clara changed trains, and now she was headed for Minneapolis. *What will my life be like here?* she wondered.

The train made its way on a trestle across a river. As Clara watched, she again remembered the Gypsy fortune-teller. How did she know Clara would cross many waters? Could she foretell the future, or were our futures preordained? Clara didn't know.

The conductor came through announcing their next stop was Minneapolis. Excitedly Clara got her bundles together. Then, following the other passengers off the train, she reached the gate. There were cries of recognition as family and friends met the passengers.

Clara walked out bravely to face her new world—alone!

Chapter 19

The North Side

The newly arrived immigrant stood there outside the Minneapolis train station, waiting. Someone was supposed to meet her here, but she didn't know if it was a man or a woman, so she looked at everybody coming by. It wasn't a good place to wait, as there was no shade and the sun's rays beat down on her head. She could even feel the heat rising from the sidewalk.

Wisps of hair wet with perspiration stuck to her forehead. She was uncomfortably warm, and her throat felt dry and parched. She wished whoever was coming would make it soon.

She saw a young man crossing the street, coming toward her. He came running, calling her name. As he came closer, her heart quickened when she recognized Usher. How good it was to see the familiar face of a friend. She could see he was happy to see her, too. He grabbed both her hands.

"Vi bist du? [How are you?]" he asked her.

"Ich been goot [I am fine]."

Usher quickly, shyly, embraced her. Her tears started and she didn't care if he saw her crying. It was as though all the anxiety of the long weeks of loneliness, bottled up inside, was finding a release through her tears.

Usher picked up her belongings. The boxes now were pretty worn, and he led her to an intersection known as Seven Corners. They were talking and looking at each other and taking note of things the same and things changed.

Usher thought, *She's even prettier than I remembered.*

Clara's assessment was, *He's just as handsome and looks older.*

Usher was carefully scrutinizing the names on the streetcars as they came along. Finally, one came and he nodded to her, saying, "Koom [come]."

The car was a "Plymouth—6th Avenue." They got on and the metal gates closed noisily behind them. Usher paid the fare and guided Clara up the aisle.

Clara sat near the open window, and as the motorman started the trolley a nice breeze came through, blowing cool on her flushed face. It felt good.

Usher's voice interrupted her thoughts. He was anxious to hear about his parents and hers. "How are they? How do they feel? What did they say?" He rattled questions off one by one.

Clara told him how his parents missed him and Liz. Clara spoke of their illnesses during the cold winters. Food and wood for heating had been short. She told how they had all shared and helped each other as much as they could.

Usher became greatly concerned. "Did they get my letters? I wrote and sent money."

Clara explained how his parents had shared a few letters, but she was sure all the mail hadn't gotten through.

Usher became angry that money he had sent that would have helped his parents was never delivered to them.

Clara explained how the situation in Romania had greatly deteriorated in the past year and everyone was suffering. She told him how hard it had been for her to leave them all. Then Clara turned her attention to the dusty city going past the trolley window. She was looking at the city through the heart of Minneapolis until it came to the North Side. That was a place noisy with the voices of bustling housewives and crying children. Other children played on the streets and sidewalks. There were the sounds of peddlers calling out their wares, wooing the women to come out and buy.

Both sides of the streets were lined with little shops, all kinds of little shops. There were two tailor shops and two grocery stores. Clara wanted to know, "Why are there two stores of everything?"

Usher explained. "If a person has a complaint against one grocer and becomes angry and doesn't like him, he can always go to the other store."

And how did Usher know this? He heard the gossip from the women coming into the bakery. He heard them complaining about the butchers. One butcher had chickens that were too fatty. The other had roasts that weren't tender. There were many complaints. Hearing all this, Usher could tell Liz which stores gave the best buys for the money.

This was a large Jewish community! Big signs and little signs, some with big Yiddish letters and others with small letters, hung crookedly in front of shops. Others, old, with their weathered paint peeling, ran straight across the tops of the storefronts. The stores were small, crowded tightly, one next to the other.

Usher pointed them out to Clara. "There is so much of everything here in a Jewish neighborhood." She couldn't believe it.

Usher took Clara across the busy street to the bakery shop. "This is where I work," he said with pride as he led her inside.

Usher introduced her to the owner, who had just finished with a customer. Mr. Rosenbloom wasn't too busy to notice Clara.

"Zie is zaher shane! [She is very pretty!]"

Usher bought a bread and they headed home. Clara was so anxious to get there to see her friend.

Liz had been waiting impatiently for them. She had run down the steps a dozen times to see if they were coming. Now, when she heard the squeaky screen door opening below, she rushed down to meet them.

The girls called out each other's name with such welcoming excitement!

"Clara!"

"Liz!"

The girls were laughing and crying, and Usher, watching, felt tears choking him, too. They had all missed someone from home. Later began the questions and answers again, and Clara and Liz found themselves interrupting each other. There was a great need to catch up—to know what they had missed in the intervening years when they were separated. It was just over two years, but they were two eventful years. Much had happened to all of them. As the girls talked, they noted with pride how each had grown up, how each had blossomed into lovely young womanhood.

Liz and Usher lived in two small rooms, sparsely furnished, each with a narrow bed, set against one wall, and a small dresser with mirror. The dressers were low and had two drawers. On top of each stood a washbasin with a pitcher, filled with water, set in it. Clara liked them very much and said so. Liz volunteered, "We bought them at a secondhand store!" Then she explained *secondhand*. She thought they had paid too much for the few pieces. "In America," she complained, "everything costs so much."

Liz's room, being a bit larger, had a two-burner gas plate set on a metal sheet on top of a wooden box. At one end of the room stood a small wooden table, with two wooden chairs. The table was covered with a rectangular cloth. Clara thought everything looked wonderful.

"Clara, you'll stay here with us until you can find a room."

"Is it all right?" Clara questioned her.

Liz said, "We talked to Mrs. Schwartz, the landlady. She lives downstairs. We can have you here for a week or two. She's charging us an extra dollar and a half a week. We'll pay it for you."

Clara was so grateful and thanked them. "As soon as I find work, I'll pay you back," she promised. It felt good being with her friends again.

Usher set Clara's belongings near Liz's bed, then went to his room to rest. Clara wanted to freshen up. She poured the cool water into the basin, then took a long drink of water from the pitcher. She washed up, splashing the water on her face and arms until she felt cool and relaxed.

Liz began preparing dinner and Clara helped set the table. She watched as Liz prepared something new, a brew made with coffee. She put water into the gray enameled pot and put in the coffee, and when the pot boiled a wonderful aroma permeated the air. Clara closed her eyes and sniffed with delight.

Liz prepared eggs, fried in butter, fresh black bread, and the coffee. Clara had never tasted coffee before. It took her a while to acquire a taste for it. It tasted so good. They were all hungry, so they ate as they talked.

"Everything is full of *tom* [taste]—the eggs, the coffee, the bread." Clara loved it all.

Liz said proudly, "Usher bakes bread just like this."

It's a miracle, Clara thought. *In Romania Usher couldn't get work. Here in America he has a job. He has learned so much. He is a baker. He can make a living for the rest of his life. Ah, dahnke Gott.* This was something important she wanted to share with her parents when she wrote them a letter.

The girls talked as they cleaned up. Liz told how life was here in America. "Mi arbit shvare un bitter far yeden tzent [we work long and hard for every cent]."

Clara talked about the escalation of troubles and problems caused by the Romanian government, the hatred for Jews, and how it had affected them all in their small area. "Sis nisht tzu voos tzi essen [there's not much to eat there]."

She worried about her parents. "Our parents wouldn't believe there's so much here for Jews. They wouldn't believe it!" Clara told her friends. Wistfully Clara wished, *If we could only send some of this food to them. How they would enjoy it.* It was useless to wish. Food could not be sent, and mail and money didn't get through most of the time.

They could have talked far into the night, but Usher reminded them he had to get up at three in the morning to get the ovens started and help set the bread. Liz, too, had to get up early to get to work.

Clara shared Liz's narrow bed. Soon she heard the steady rhythmic breathing of a sleeping Liz, but she couldn't sleep.

It had been a most exciting day—being reunited with her friends and seeing so many nice things around the community.

Clara was comparing what Liz and Usher had here in America to what they had in Romania. Even though they complained about hard work and little pay and how expensive things were, to Clara, knowing the worsened conditions that existed in Romania, everything here was better. If they complained again, she would remind them of several things they had to be grateful for: They were Jews and had jobs. They had a nice place to stay, without worrying about government interference. They were in a land that was free. When Clara had walked the area with Usher that day, there were no soldiers, and the people didn't look sad and frightened. That was it! She didn't see fear in the faces of the people here. She thought of Liz and Usher and herself; they had all grown up so much. They had become young adults! Liz and Usher were now living the day-to-day experiences in America. It was a struggle. They didn't escape the struggle, but they were free.

Now Clara, too, had come this far distance ready to take on the struggle. She wished she could talk to her parents to tell them how it really was here. They had sent her away fearing for her life. They wanted her to have a chance at a better life to be free!

Now Clara was free. She didn't know yet what that would mean for her. All she knew was they had all paid a great price—separation from family. But there was promise here. With that thought in mind, she fell asleep.

The next day at the bakery Usher's boss, Mr. Rosenbloom, had to remind him twice that the bread was ready to come out of the oven.

"Vie is dein kopf heint? [Where is your head today?] Seh miz zein mit die greeneh [it must be with the newcomer]."

Mr. Rosenbloom hit the nail right on the head. Usher's thoughts were with Clara. She had always been a pretty girl, but now she was a beautiful young woman. Anyone could see that. That wasn't all of it. It was the kind of warm, kind person she was. He knew that, too.

Here in America, Usher had been introduced to many young women who came into the shop. Anxious mothers were always on the lookout for a *shidduch,* and Mr. Rosenbloom was willing to help them for a fee. Mothers began sending their daughters, of all shapes and sizes, to the bakery when they heard there was a nice-looking, fine Jewish boy there. This made business good for Mr. Rosenbloom, as some came in two or three times a day to buy bread. The mothers knew this was a good investment, but Mr. Rosenbloom wondered, *What do they do with all the bread?*

Mothers came and asked Usher to dinner. (Some even included his sister, Liz.) The dinners were good, but he always came away from these encounters feeling very stressed and unhappy. He didn't know why; then he would think of Clara. None of the girls had Clara's ways. She was a caring, kindhearted person, and she had a good, sensible head. As Usher put it to Liz, "Zie is balbotish [she is refined]."

He had missed her and was overjoyed when he learned she was coming to America. Now here she was!

Mr. Rosenbloom gave him a few hours off so he could take her for some interviews at places a Jewish organization had arranged.

Ladies' fashions at this time were beautiful blouses and dresses made of the finest fabrics. There was a great demand for fine seamstresses in shops and factories in what was known as the needle-and-thread trade.

One of Clara's interviews included a test of hand-sewing the finishing touches on a collar on a silk dress. She got the job the following week. She did all the fine hand-stitching on the most delicate fabrics, like silks, georgettes, and fine linens. It was painstaking work, but she sewed with the skill of an artist, as her mother and Gittel had taught her. Her finishing techniques were admired by all. Soon they called her "the one with golden fingers." She was paid by the piece and was in demand for the extra fine work, which kept her busy constantly.

Each girl was given a quota every day and had to finish it and sometimes even do extra pieces or lose her job. Sometimes the young women were ill and couldn't finish their quotas. They helped each other out, skipping their fifteen-minute lunch breaks and doing the extra pieces. They all needed this support system at one time or another. All did it willingly.

Clara had to get up early to catch the streetcar that took her from Plymouth north to work in downtown Minneapolis. The day began early and ended late. The workers had to stay over whenever an order had to be gotten out.

Working conditions were far from good. In summer the rooms were too warm and the girls left their sewing tables only once during the day—for a drink of water. Lighting was better in summer. Light came in the small windows and made it easier to see what they were sewing.

In the winter the lighting was very poor. Ceiling lights hung down, but not far enough. One bulb hanging from an electric cord didn't cast much light. The room was cold, warmed by one heater in a far corner.

Clara said years later, "My feet were so cold, I couldn't feel them to push down the pedal on the sewing machine."

Sometimes the girls' fingers were so cold, they could hardly hold the needles. Clara's eyes were becoming strained, and she had great difficulty seeing in the winter.

One day, Mr. Gold, one of the bosses, came into the sewing room. He stomped around, shouting at the supervisor and chomping furiously on his cigar. The girls were behind on the order, and he wanted it out that afternoon.

The day was very dark and dreary, and the lighting did absolutely no good at all. Mr. Gold stopped in front of Clara's table and watched her. She became nervous and dropped her needle and couldn't find it on the floor.

He yelled, "Can't you find it?"

Clara said, "No. The lighting isn't too good." Clara stood up to ask for another needle.

Mr. Gold became red in the face. He was so angry the words sputtered from his mouth. He told her in no uncertain terms, "No one ever complained before, and if you can't do the work, we'll get someone else who can."

He shook his finger in Clara's face, embarrassing her and frightening her. She was sure she was going to lose her job and worried the rest of the day.

Clara didn't lose her job, but she learned never to complain again. She learned in America there weren't too many opportunities for immigrant women. Women were too frightened to say anything and took abuse in many forms—poor working conditions, low wages, long, long hours, irregular or no lunch periods, and bosses who were slave drivers and greedy. The places of employment were sweatshops!

Clara felt she was fortunate to have her job. She hadn't been here very long and was trying to learn the language and make her own living. She began to save nickels. With every nickel, she felt a nail was hammered to form another rung of a ladder she hoped would someday get her out of the shop, to something better. She would work and learn.

There was hope in her heart. Here in America a person could work and hope for anything he or she wanted. Thus started a love affair—Clara with her America—that lasted all her life!

Chapter 20
Life with the Kaplans

Clara stayed with the Solomons for a week, but brother and sister got into frequent arguments, making it uncomfortable for Clara. They searched for another place, and Clara was fortunate to find a room with the Kaplan family, who usually rented to an immigrant boarder. Their house was located on Girard Avenue North, just a few blocks from the Solomons. In fact, there was a shortcut through the yards across the street. The worn path was evidence that it was used frequently, even though a rusted old sign with "NO TRESPASS-ING—PRIVATE PROPERTY" hung there.

The house was fair-sized, with a porch and a wonderful wood swing. Inside, the house was furnished adequately, with rug-covered wood floors and pictures on the wall. There was a wedding picture of the Kaplans, not smiling, but looking handsome in their fine clothes. They had married very young and years of hard work and raising a family had taken their toll, and now the Kaplans were not the young couple anymore.

A wedding picture must be something special in a home, Clara thought. To her mind it was a very important thing to have in a home. It gave the home and family—well, she couldn't explain it, but it was a special feeling. Here at the Kaplans' it was a feeling of security. Their home was a safe haven.

The Kaplans had three daughters, and Clara shared a room with Ida. She was only a year older than Clara and already had a steady boyfriend, named Louis. The other daughters—Sarah, twelve, and Anna, eight—were typical youngsters, sometimes obedient, sometimes belligerent, but fun to be with. They shared a bedroom across the narrow hall in the upstairs of the home.

Clara had been in Minneapolis just over three weeks. Already she had a job and had moved twice. Here she was living with a new family, a houseful of strangers to get used to. She was nervous and frightened and worried whether they would like her enough to let her stay. Since leaving her home, she had been on the move for a long time, a displaced person who desperately wanted to belong somewhere and not move again.

Clara and the Kaplans could converse in Yiddish, but all the while the Kaplans tried to teach their boarder English. She listened intently to anyone speaking the language—people at work, in the shop, and on the streetcar. She tried to figure out what they were saying and in this way learned a little more each day.

The two younger Kaplan girls laughed at the way "the *greeneh* [immigrant]" pronounced words with her foreign accent. To them it was funny, but Clara felt ashamed and discouraged that other young people could speak it and she couldn't. It was frustrating to her when she tried to put together a sentence and couldn't make herself understood.

Ida, more patient and understanding, scolded her younger sisters: "How would you feel if you had to leave your home and family and come to a new land where you didn't understand what people were saying to you? Would you like to be laughed at by idiots like you two?" The girls couldn't even imagine themselves in that situation. No one here would make them leave their home. But they came to a better understanding of what Clara was going through. They really liked her and often talked about how nice she was to have in their home. They knew they had not been so lucky with other boarders quite a few times. Clara was a friendly, vivacious person, anxious to learn, even little things. She was fascinated by how they folded their clothes and put them in drawers. She had one drawer in a dresser, and soon she was folding her few belongings the same way. Every day was a learning experience for Clara and when they nodded their approval, she was so pleased. They came to respect her effort to learn the American way of doing things.

During the week, the family had dinner together, but many nights hardworking Mr. Kaplan didn't make it home until very late. No matter how late it was, Mrs. Kaplan would come down and serve him the dinner that had been kept warm in the oven. But on Friday night Mr. Kaplan always came home early. That was one night the family was all together.

Dinner was a pleasant affair, with the girls laughing or talking. Sometimes they teased each other. Many times there were good-natured fun-loving exchanges between them, and other times there was the bickering of siblings. Most of the time they got along fairly well!

In one corner of the living room stood an upright piano, and many times after dinner Ida would play it. Clara had never seen or heard one. Ida let Clara sit beside her on the cushioned piano bench, and Clara would feel so honored. She thought Ida was the most wonderful person, because she could put her fingers on the black and white keys and make such beautiful music. The girls stood around and sang Yiddish and American songs, and Clara sang along as soon as she learned the songs. When they heard her join in with her lovely voice they applauded her effort, which encouraged her. She would never forget how good they were to her when she needed their warmth and support.

Louis came courting one night a week, usually after dinner. Sometimes he was invited for a Friday night's special dinner. The younger sisters were always forewarned to be on their best behavior.

Ida became very excited when Louis was coming. She kept changing things around in the living room, where the couple always sat. She would take the pillows from the davenport and put them somewhere else. Then she'd cock her head this way and that, shake her head no, then put them back. She changed the pictures on top of the piano two or three times, then changed the bowl on the lace runner on the dining room table. Dissatisfied, she then hurried to put it all back again and barely made it before he was there knocking at the door. Her face was always flushed as she eagerly went to open it.

Louis always brought a bag of candy for the girls and a small box of her favorite chocolates for Ida. Everyone in the neighborhood knew Ida and Louis were "a *poor* [pair]" going together. Sometimes they went to a show; then other times they went for long walks in the park.

When they came back to sit on the swing, they had first choice above everybody else. The younger ones balked when told they had to leave and questioned, "Why?"

Mrs. Kaplan gave them the same answer every time: "When you're older, you'll know why. Now just go and let them be."

The young ones knew then, *No more questions!* and went in.

In the evening Mr. Kaplan sat relaxed, reading his Jewish paper. The paper was noted for a famous column devoted to the readers who wrote of their love troubles, family problems, things wrong at work, and hundreds of other poignant stories. Mr. Kaplan would read them aloud and also the advice given by the columnist. There were always some who agreed and some who disagreed with the advice given, and this started some lively discussions among the family. It was always good, and Clara listened and learned. There was a great deal to learn about people.

Mrs. Kaplan did mending or just sat resting, enjoying the family, her face beaming with pride.

Clara loved these evenings with family together and missed

hers. How she wished they could be with her now! Life in America was different in some respects, but when it came to loving family, it was the same as in her village in Vaslui. Clara saw this in the Kaplan family and felt so blessed that she had found a wonderful place like this to live.

Mrs. Kaplan when she spoke of Clara said, "Zie is azai tzegelast [she is such a warm, loving person]."

The Kaplans certainly made her feel welcome and included her in everything they did. She was like one of their own. They were a family struggling to raise their children in America.

Mr. Kaplan took his old horse and wagon out early every morning. He traveled around all day in all kinds of weather, through all kinds of neighborhoods, buying old furniture. Sometimes he came home with stories of how in some neighborhoods they made fun of him and his horse and wagon, even throwing stones at them. He didn't go there again.

The old furniture was kept in the barn in back of the house. His work days were long and tiring and back-breaking, but he never complained.

On Sundays he got up early and set the furniture out in the backyard, where people came through the alley and haggled about prices. Some looked and left without buying anything, while others stayed and purchased a piece or two. Much of it was sold to *greeneh* who were starting new lives here.

Many came to buy even though they had very little money. He let them take what they needed, with the promise to pay him back a dollar a month. It took a long time to pay for things at that rate.

Once in a while he found someone who didn't honor his promise to pay, which made Mr. Kaplan angry. He counted on that money for his family. He would discuss the situation at dinner, not mentioning names, but impressing on his children and Clara the importance of paying one's debts. Doing that was obeying one of the Ten Commandments: "Thou shalt not steal." Keeping money that belonged to others was stealing. It was important to be honest.

Saturday mornings Mr. Kaplan took his tallith and went to the synagogue. After services, on the way home, he had discussions with the other men about happenings in the world. One thing they were all interested in was the warring countries in Europe. Everyone had somebody left behind in one country or another. War over there was a topic of great concern to all. Clara, listening, worried about her parents.

Clara had come away from her home with a deep sense of who

she was. She cherished her heritage as a Jew and was always mindful of the customs and traditions handed down to her in her religion.

Clara remembered her first Friday night *erev shabbos* (before the Sabbath) at the Kaplans'. She sat at the table and watched as Mrs. Kaplan covered her head with a folded napkin, then held her hands over the lighted candles and said the ancient prayer. Tears came to Clara's eyes as she remembered seeing her dear mother and her dear Gittel doing the same. To herself she began the prayer: *Baruch attah Adonai elohenu melech h'olam asher kiddeshanu b'mitzvotav vetzivanu l'hadlik ner shel Shabbat* [blessed art Thou, O Lord, our God, king of the universe, who has sanctified us by Thy commandments and instructed us to kindle the Sabbath lights]. Then a special *Shabbos* dinner was served. After that dinner, Clara felt closer to the Kaplans. Here in America they became her family.

Clara learned to knit and crochet and soon designed a sweater. She made her first one as a gift to Ida, who was amazed at the talent this young girl had. When the other sisters saw it, they wanted sweaters, too. Clara promised to make them when she had some spare time.

She was very creative and made so many different styles of different colors and special trims. Each one was unique.

The news of Clara's sweaters spread, and soon she was asked to take orders because so many people wanted them. Clara learned where to get the yarn wholesale; she did the work in the evenings and from then on always made herself extra money. She could depend on herself to do it!

Work! Work! Work! That was the busy schedule of the week. Once in a while Ida, Liz, and Clara went to an early evening movie at the neighborhood show. They sat and watched the great lovers of the screen and fantasized about loves of their own. It sometimes helped the boredom of the workweek.

Ida and Clara walked Liz home, then cut across the yards, taking the shortcut home.

Sometimes when the late summer nights were balmy, with clear skies and hundreds of stars twinkling down, they didn't go in right away but sat on the swing. It was beautiful and quiet out, and their hearts, eager and young, yearned for what they knew not.

When fall came, they went out into the cool, crisp air with their faces snuggled into warm coat collars. They walked along streets dark except for the dim gas-lit street lamps, which cast eerie shadows on the walks. Then home they would hurry to talk about the boys, events of the day, and what would happen tomorrow.

It was the fall of 1912, and Clara had been here six months.

On winter nights, they stayed home, often sipping hot cocoa. Ida played the piano, and they sang or sat around the stove, with red-hot coals crackling and burning in its belly, and felt the warmth of the togetherness of family.

Sometimes Clara finished up a sweater someone had ordered. There was always something to do, and life went on.

Chapter 21

The Foursome

On the north side, the Sabbath was strictly observed by all Jewish-owned stores on Plymouth Avenue, and that was almost every shop. They were closed from sundown Friday to after sundown Saturday. This meant most men and boys attended services at the different shuls (synagogues) in the neighborhood.

After services, most hurried home for lunch and rest. Others lingered awhile for discussions about the politics of the shul. There was always disagreement with the way the affairs of the synagogue were managed, which led to heated discussions. Arguments were never settled but carried forward from one Sabbath to the next, until a new administration was appointed. Then the discussions began all over again.

Time spent at the shul was also a social time for men to discuss problems of the week, their work, their struggles, and even a little gossip. Yes, men gossip—not in the same way as women do, but it was there.

For the young men this was an opportunity to meet others, especially the "new ones" (the immigrants). Usher was helped immeasurably when he became affiliated with his shul. It gave him a feeling of belonging.

In the few years Usher had been here, there were numerous opportunities for him to become acquainted with several young men. Many had been in his same predicament, newcomers and alone. They therefore could empathize with him.

Sometimes, when he had been desperately lonely, Usher accepted an invitation to dinner. He went with much misgiving, since he found it extremely difficult going to different homes to sit and eat and attempt to carry on a conversation with strangers.

When Liz came, things changed for the better. That is, they were better for a while. The first year, the two got along fairly well. The second year, things changed. There were moments of great tension between them, and they quarrelled a lot. Liz cried and was unhappy, and Usher was frustrated. He became short-tempered and angry. The fighting stopped when he left the house. That was his way of coping with the problem. He avoided it.

94

Neither one could answer, Why? Why was this happening?

Each one was always tired. Being tired was their plausible explanation of the situation. They often heard others say they were always tired. Tired must come with being in America!

One *Shabbos* Usher met a young man named Sol Sadoff. The two became inseparable friends. They seemed to have so much in common. They carried on long discussions about work, the shul, and other things. All in all, they got along remarkably well.

They had been friends for over a year, and Usher wanted to have Sol over. He invited Clara and Sol for a Sunday dinner. When the girls questioned Usher about Sol, he was rather vague. After all, how does one young man describe another? Usher judged by how Sol *davened* (said his prayers) in the shul. According to how he did that, to Usher, "He is a very fine person!" The girls had no idea what to expect.

Sunday finally rolled around. Clara came earlier to help, and there was much going on in the small kitchen-bedroom. It was a warm summer day, and the heat from the two-burner gas plate didn't help much. Dinner was almost ready, and they were awaiting the arrival of the other guest.

Liz asked Usher, "What time did you tell him to come?"

Usher said he wasn't sure. He thought he said five-thirty; then he said, "Maybe I said six o'clock." He didn't remember.

Clara was uncomfortably warm. "It's past five-forty-five. Where is he?" she asked.

Liz answered her with, "He probably forgot and isn't coming. We'll wait a few more minutes, and if he's not here, we'll eat."

Usher was getting angry at their impatience and went down to wait for his friend. After what seemed like an eternity but was only ten minutes, the girls heard the voices of Usher and his friend as they came up the stairs. The girls were unprepared for the most pleasant surprise. Liz's face became more flushed than it already was as she took in this good-looking, rather dapper, tall, thin chap with his shock of brown hair. They all stood there as the formalities of introduction were gotten out of the way. Then they sat—as there wasn't too much room to maneuver in.

At the table, when Sol looked up at Liz, she blushed. He thought, *What a lovely sister Usher has, and all this time he never said too much about her. Brothers! Go figure them!*

It didn't take a genius to tell the two were attracted to each other.

Sol had heard Usher talk about his Clara many, many times, and now he could understand why Usher felt the way he did. Clara

95

was all Usher had described and more. She was beautiful and had a most pleasant demeanor and Sol particularly liked her warm smile. He noticed, too, that Usher couldn't keep his eyes off her.

Dinner was simple, hamburgers and mashed potatoes, the best the girls could do on the two-burner gas plate. Clara had brought Mrs. Kaplan's homemade kosher pickles, and there was lemonade and cookies. The lemonade wasn't too cold, as the ice had already melted, but no one seemed to mind.

The dinner met with the approval of all and was a huge success—probably helped by Cupid, who must have been flitting among them, resting on each shoulder and watching the chaos he was creating.

The boys went downstairs while the girls cleaned up. Liz confided to Clara, "I have never seen such a handsome young man." Of course, to Clara that was debatable, since she thought Usher fit that description, but she didn't argue with her friend.

The girls finished the cleanup, freshened up, and went down. The men ended their conversation abruptly when they saw the girls. The evening was young and there was much to look forward to. They decided to walk to the park, not too far away, and paired off, Sol and Liz in front, and Clara and Usher behind them.

"I think they like each other," Usher whispered to Clara.

"Wouldn't that be wonderful?" Clara's voice was full of excitement for her friend.

"I'd be a *shotkin* [matchmaker]. Can you believe that?" Usher was full of wonderment at the possibility.

At the park they found a bench and sat and talked for a while; then at times they were quiet—just people-watching. It was warm and the girls waved their handkerchiefs, using them as fans to create a slight breeze. The boys, too, were warm and rolled up their shirt sleeves.

Clara volunteered the information that the Kaplans had gone on a picnic given by an organization to which Mr. Kaplan belonged. "Come back to the house. We can have some lemonade and cookies." She took Usher's arm and they got up.

The boys sat on the swing and the girls brought out the refreshments. In summer guests were always offered cool lemonade. It was a sign of hospitality. Clara pretended she was the lady of the house, pouring the lemonade from the pitcher into tall glasses, then passing them to her guests. It was cool and refreshing, and Usher told her so. Her face glowed when he looked at her.

Sol liked the cookies and helped himself to one, then another, and still another, until they were gone.

Lights came on in the house. The Kaplans had returned. One by one they came traipsing out to see who was on the porch. Mrs. Kaplan called from the kitchen, "Is Clara home yet?"

Mrs. Kaplan came out and wanted to know how the dinner was, since Clara had taken her hamburger recipe. The Kaplans related different happenings that had taken place at the picnic. They all had a wonderful time. Mr. Kaplan, usually not very talkative, excitedly told them, "There were so many people out there. A lot of money must have been made." This made him extremely happy, because his organization used the money to help newly arrived immigrants.

"Thank God," he said. "The picnic was a huge success!"

The two couples were left on the swing. The talk turned to many things, and then to "wishes."

They all wished they had a lot of money. They could buy so many things and do so many good things—bring their parents over to America. Usher wished the coming week of work was over and it was Sunday again. The girls wished they didn't have to get up so early to go to work. It was getting late and Sol wished he didn't live so far away so he could stay longer. With that, he got up to go.

"Come. I'll take you home," he said to Liz.

They said their good nights and walked down the steps, just as the lamplighter came up the street. There were not too many people out; everyone was tired from the picnic.

Everything was quiet, except for the chirping of the crickets, and Clara and Usher watched the lamplighter as he lighted the gas lamps first on one side of the street, then on the other.

"We had such a wonderful time today, Usher. Everybody was feeling good, and we were all happy. I wish it could always be like this."

"Why shouldn't it be?" he asked, a bit puzzled.

She hesitated a moment, then in a reflective mood answered, "I don't know."

"You worry too much." Then he added, "I'm glad you're my girl. Ich liebe dier [I love you]."

He kissed her gently and got up to go. "I wonder if Sol left yet?"

This time it was Clara who remarked, "Did you see how happy Liz was? I know she likes him."

Usher speculated, "Wouldn't it be something if he became my brother-in-law?"

"Well, we will just have to wait and see," said Clara.

They said their good nights, and Usher started off on a run across the street, taking the shortcut home, and Clara went in.

The day had been perfect and she wished it didn't have to end. These were delightful days—simple times with simple pleasures.

Every Saturday night was date night, and the two couples, Liz and Sol, and Clara and Usher, went to the neighborhood theater. The boys sometimes got a little too bold in the darkness of the show and held the girls' hands. Clara would look around, so worried someone would see them. Girls had to be careful of their reputations.

After the show, they strolled down Plymouth Avenue to the corner drugstore or the ice-cream shop, whichever one wasn't too crowded. They sat and sipped five-cent cherry or chocolate phosphates, sipping them slowly to make them last longer.

The girls let the boys finish first. If the girls finished first, the boys would have to ask if they wanted another, and the boys could not afford more than the show and the five-cent phosphate or ice cream. The girls finished last and the boys with their best manners asked them, anyway, if they would like another. No matter how hot and thirsty they were, the girls politely refused, said they were really quite full, and thanked the young men.

On a lovely summer's evening they walked around the neighborhood, alive with shops opened up after Sabbath sundown. They met other friends and sometimes stopped and chatted, but mostly they enjoyed being together.

Sometimes, if they weren't too tired walking, they made it to the neighborhood park. The boys had taken the girls there on their first date, and it became their favorite place. They found benches and sat and talked of work, people, and themselves. Clara, Liz, and Usher talked of home in Romania, and Sol listened and learned about the three of them and their struggles. Sol told of his parents working hard in a grocery store. He had many brothers and sisters. Life was a struggle for them, too.

Sol said, "Jews struggle here. We work hard."

Clara said, "That's true, but here you have a chance to work. That's a big thing. That's something we didn't have."

Clara felt her life was much different, but better—so much better—here in America. She loved her life, struggle and all, and she loved America!

Clara, like Liz, had "*zech ois ge greent* [become Americanized]." This was the ultimate goal of all immigrants. They worked hard to achieve it, but it was more difficult for some than for others. To be labeled a "greenhorn" (an immigrant who wasn't picking up the American way) was the worst possible insult. Everyone wanted to look like an American.

It wasn't difficult for Clara. Soon she was able to purchase a few of the American fashions. She had a knack for selecting things that looked exceptionally good on her.

She wore the new pencil-slim skirts and lovely shirtwaists that showed off her shapely figure, and shoes with pointed toes and high heels. Usher always complimented her and told her how beautiful she looked, which made her blush but feel wonderful. Always clean and neat and feminine-looking, she had an air of refinement about her and a charm that turned heads wherever she went. She was happy and becoming accustomed to life in America!

After a night out, the two couples would eventually head back to the Kaplans' house. Mr. and Mrs. Kaplan were usually sitting on the porch swing, enjoying a little much-deserved relaxation. They were wonderfully understanding people. Remembering their youth, Mr. Kaplan would speak up.

"Dora, it's late. Let's go in." Then he yawned, and they both said their good nights and went in, relinquishing the much-sought-after swing to the young people. They never got angry at the two couples using the swing as if they owned it.

The two couples sat so cramped together they could hardly breathe, but when you're young and in love these trivial things just don't matter. Sol's right arm was wedged in so tightly he had difficulty trying to extricate it to light a cigarette, Liz was snuggled so close to him. Usher sat next, with Clara squeezed against his chest, but there were no complaints.

They talked little, thinking their own thoughts, dreaming their own dreams, content to be where they were, each young man with his girl. They had many wonderful evenings like this.

One night, with a sigh, Sol spoke up; it was getting late. "Lizzie," as he now called Liz, "come, I'll take you home."

Sol always left first. He had a long ride home on the trolley— almost to the end of the line. He said he didn't mind, as he always managed to catch a *driml* (nap) on the streetcar.

Usher secretly welcomed their departure. It gave Clara and him more room on the swing, for one thing, and a little more privacy, for another. The foursome was together on almost all their dates. Usher felt he didn't get enough time alone with Clara, and he was sure Sol felt the same way about Liz.

When at last they were alone, Usher and Clara discussed what they expected to get out of their lives.

Clara had thought about it. She wanted to be married someday and have a place of her own and children. She wanted a family. That was important to her.

"All women want the same thing," Usher said. "The trouble is they don't have to worry. The man has to worry about everything—work, taking care of his wife and family and all other expenses. That's a big worry!"

Clara retorted with, "All husbands have to do that."

Yet Usher wanted the same things Clara did; a place of his own and a family.

Later, as she lay in bed going over the almost perfect summer day, she reflected on the conversation with Usher and his feelings. Sometimes she didn't understand him. Perhaps all young men felt the same way. That was something she wanted to question Liz about, Sol's feelings on the subject.

Chapter 22

Marriage

When the boys walked home from the synagogue, they discussed, among other things, the women in their lives. Usher had confided to Sol that he was planning to marry Clara.

Young people, thinking of marriage at this time and in this place didn't have financial security. They were lucky to have their jobs, and the pay wasn't too much. For the poor, opportunities for advancement were nil. Once they were married, though, there was a commitment to the marriage and each other. It was a struggle, but they survived in the patriarchal society.

Usher spent many nights working out a budget for the expenses he felt would be incurred when he and Clara were married. It was one of the things he discussed with Sol, as if Sol could solve the problem.

"I look at Lazer, the other baker; he makes the same amount of money I do. He's married and doesn't seem to have a worry in the world. If he can manage, why shouldn't I?"

Sol shrugged his shoulders. What could he say to Usher? He himself didn't know too much about the subject. He listened to his older brothers, Usher, and his other friends and was glad he didn't have to make any decisions about it just yet.

All that week Usher battled himself about the pros and cons of marriage expenses, although the fear of taking the step into matrimony may have had something to do with it. At any rate, he had many doubts, but by the end of week, when he met Sol again, he had done an excellent job of dispelling his fears and had convinced himself he and Clara could manage. When he spoke to his friend, it was with a renewed confidence.

"I know we will be all right. Now, what about you, Sol?"

"No." Sol shook his head. "I can't think of marriage for another few years."

"Why?"

Sol didn't offer any explanation, as though closing the subject. Usher wanted to press on with it. He had a sudden twinge; he wondered if Liz knew this.

In December, Jews on the North Side, like Jews everywhere, were celebrating Hanukkah, the Festival of Lights. It was the night of "the First Candle," when gifts were sometimes exchanged. Usher was coming over. When he and Clara were alone in the living room, he presented her with a little box. She opened it to find an exquisitely carved cameo pin. She was deeply touched by its daintiness and beauty. Usher pinned it at the neckline of her shirtwaist, and she fingered it lovingly.

He had searched for something special for her. He wanted this to be a special night, one she would always remember. He was pleased that she had admired his choice of a gift for her. Of course, the Kaplans had to come in and see it and all agreed it was quite a wonderful piece of jewelry.

Usher thought he and Clara should go for a walk. Clara was hesitant.

"It's so cold out." Clara shuddered but got her coat out.

Usher helped her with her galoshes, and she pulled her coat collar up so only the tip of her nose showed, and off they went.

The cold December air was brisk, and the dark sky shone with bright stars as they walked down the block, both happy and laughing, as their teeth chattered when they tried to speak.

They made it only once around the block, then went in, feeling wonderfully refreshed. There was one light on in the living room, and the Hanukkah candle in the menorah on the dining room table was still burning.

Usher said, "Clara, I have to ask you something."

"What?" she wanted to know, as she took her hat off. She could see he was nervous.

"Will you marry me?" Usher finally got it out.

Clara remembered how the breath caught in her throat. Usher had told her numerous times that he loved her. He said it again now: "Ich liebe dier."

When she thought about it later, she couldn't describe her feelings. She was happy and excited, yes, but also apprehensive.

When the girls talked of being married, they imagined Ida would be the first, then Liz, and then Clara. She was, after all, the youngest. Now here she was, the first getting the proposal of marriage. She felt warm and tingly all over and knew, if he looked at her, she was blushing.

Clara had not answered Usher, and he began to get fidgety. What if she said no? He had been so sure of himself, he had not imagined

102

the possibility of a refusal. Now, he was almost afraid of her answer. It could be: "No!"

Clara, unaware of this turmoil within him, looked at him, nodded her head, and answered him, "Yes." She never thought to say no. Wasn't this what was expected of girls, to marry, have families, and take care of them? She was going to do all of that.

Usher had gotten up the courage to ask her. Now it was done. He felt a great sense of relief. Usher kissed her gently, then left to tell Liz.

Such wonderful news had to be shared with someone. Clara gently shook Ida awake.

"What is it? What is it?" Ida asked, her voice clearly sounding her concern. When she heard the news, she excitedly jumped out of bed. "Mazel tov! Congratulations!" Then she voiced the prayer of young women everywhere: "I hope it will be me soon."

The next morning Clara was up before Mrs. Kaplan, she was so anxious to tell her the good news. Mrs. Kaplan hugged and kissed her, but she did say, "You're so young, Clara, so young."

Now there was the excitement of the engagement period. Everyone was happy for them: "Two such fine people, they deserve the best."

Usher got *mazel tovs* at the bakery. Mr. Rosenbloom put out a decanter of kosher wine and glasses, and all who came into the shop that day toasted the groom-to-be. Of course, Mr. Rosenbloom knew he would lose some business from disappointed mothers and daughters now that Usher, the eligible bachelor, was no longer on the matchmaking block.

Liz came over to congratulate Clara. Now they weren't only friends but soon would be sisters-in-law!

When Usher and Clara made wedding plans, Clara worried about Liz. What would she do? It was decided Liz would live with them in another, larger place. Liz would help with the rent and her share of the expenses. Secretly Liz hoped it wouldn't be too much longer before she and Sol would be married and have a place of their own. Neither Liz nor Clara knew Sol couldn't plan to be married for a few years.

The year was 1913. In America, President Taft went out as the twenty-seventh president and Woodrow Wilson was elected the twenty-eighth.

In April 1913 the wedding of Clara and Usher was held at the Kaplans'. Mr. Kaplan had the rabbi of his shul perform the ceremony. The Kaplans stood in for Clara's parents. It was a small wedding, with the Kaplans, Usher's boss and his wife, Clara's boss and his wife, Liz, Sol, and a few friends.

They say, "All brides are beautiful," but Clara was an exceptionally lovely bride. Everyone said so! Her dress of white satin was form-fitting and ankle-length. The bodice had tiny satin-covered buttons marching down the front, from the high neck to the waist. The sleeves were tight-fitting, elbow-length, and she wore fine long, white leather gloves and white leather shoes. Her face was pink with excitement, and she wore her long brown hair pulled back and pinned up high and covered with a long, lovely veil. She carried a very small bouquet of tiny white roses. She made a breathtaking picture.

Usher was quite handsome in his new suit, and there was a photographer to take a few pictures of the bride and groom. Clara wanted a wedding picture to hang on the wall of their home.

Ida played the "Wedding March" as Clara came down the stairs. The couple looked so young, innocents! She was eighteen, and he was twenty-one. They stood straight and tall under the marriage *chupa.*

Mrs. Kaplan had prepared a dinner for the guests. Mr. Rosenbloom made them a special wedding cake. Mrs. Kaplan gave them a pair of beautiful candlesticks, *Shabbos* candlesticks, and they got other wonderful wedding presents.

"How wonderful people are." Clara couldn't believe how good people were to her and Usher.

Parents wait a long time to see their children grown and married. Mrs. Kaplan began to cry. Her thoughts were with the couple's parents in Romania. If they had not received the letters telling them about the wedding, they did not know their children were being married that day and could not share in their happiness. All that day, whenever Mrs. Kaplan thought about the cruelty overseas that brought about this sadness she would start to sob.

Clara and Usher were very happy on their wedding day, as all brides and grooms should be on this, the most important day in their lives.

The couple were so grateful to the Kaplans and thanked them for their beautiful wedding. Mrs. Kaplan embraced Clara. "You're like my own daughter," she said in Yiddish. "How could I let you go without a nice wedding?"

Clara and Usher sent letters to their parents telling them about the wedding. There was no way to know if the letters were received.

If they were, the families in Romania learned they were now *macha-toonim* (in-laws).

Liz stayed with Ida that night. Full of hope, young, and so in love and nervous, Clara and Usher went back to his place, to begin their married life. For the moment Usher's doubts about marriage disappeared. He and his love forgot about tomorrow. What would the tomorrows bring? Who could say?

Chapter 23
Life with the Solomons

After much deliberating and planning, the newlyweds and Liz moved into a three-room apartment, the upper part of a duplex. This, they felt, they could manage, with Clara working and Liz paying her share of the expenses.

Usher and Liz brought their few pieces of furniture, and the bride and groom added their wedding gifts. Clara set her *Shabbos* candlesticks on the table, and the place took on a warm, homey feeling.

In time, Clara was able to purchase a secondhand Singer sewing machine from Mr. Kaplan and made the curtains for the different rooms, which made the apartment look even nicer. The young newly marrieds were deliriously happy with their first home. If you asked them, they would have told you, "Married life is wonderful!"

They felt like rich folk when they added their few wedding gifts of money to the bank account Clara had started with her nickels. "Can you imagine having money in an American bank?" She was ecstatic!

Clara had been so proud when she took her savings passbook with her money to deposit at the bank. She waited patiently while the teller behind the glass cubicle counted it, then put it in a drawer and marked it carefully in her book. Clara always checked it to see if he had written the correct amount. Little by little the total increased, making her feel important. There wasn't much in the account, but they were determined to add to it regularly. Usher and Clara had talked about it, and they were of the opinion that it was important to have even a small cushion to fall back on, in case of an emergency or illness.

They bought a small icebox that didn't hold more than ten cents' worth of ice and were careful shoppers, buying only what they needed, so nothing was wasted. Usher insisted on this.

It seemed they waited a long time for their wedding pictures to come, but finally they did arrive. Clara and Usher were impatient to open them. They were almost as excited as children opening gifts. Then she saw them and couldn't believe how wonderful they were. They scrutinized them at close range and then held them an arm's length away, then checked them ever so carefully, Clara pointing out her white shoes and gloves and Usher touching his tie.

People look at themselves in the mirror and see themselves in different ways. They are always surprised when they see themselves in pictures, and it's never the way they imagine themselves. So it was with Clara and Usher; they never thought they would look like this finished product. They showed the pictures around proudly to their friends and one and all agreed they were, indeed, a very handsome couple.

The Kaplans received a picture and all "ohed" and "ahed"; then Mrs. Kaplan put it in a place of honor on top of the piano in the living room.

Liz also got one and put it on top of her dresser. She gazed at it longingly, and Clara, watching, understood.

"I know you will have your own soon, real soon." She looked at Liz encouragingly.

Usher and Clara had one larger picture made and put it in a handsome oval frame. It hung on the wall in their bedroom. Clara sat on the bed and gazed at it.

"Someday," she said, "when we have a living room, it will hang there." Her heart was gladdened with the prospect of what that represented to her—a stable home and a family, a place secure with love.

They had two more pictures, and those were sent off to their parents in Romania, even though the couple was uncertain whether they would be received. The 1913 war between Romania and Bulgaria had begun, and this caused them grave concern.

In the honeymoon apartment, the couple, very much in love, were happy, and the honeymoon days were sweet!

All in all, things were working out exceedingly well. Clara and Liz, as always, got along together, sharing the duties of the household. There was no serious problem. However, quite often Liz and Usher got into a wrangle about something or other, and Usher always complained about his hours at work. The times were hard, and they lived frugally and managed with their plan to save a little every week. But even the best-laid plans often go awry.

On a morning in May, Clara became ill, but she went in to work. Missing a day of work meant a smaller paycheck, and they couldn't afford that.

The following morning Clara was still ill, and this time, try as she might, it was impossible for her to make it out of bed.

Usher and Liz had already gone to work. Clara, terribly frightened, remembering her mother's illness, went to Mrs. Kaplan. A teakettle bubbled over the gas flame, and Mrs. Kaplan served them each a cup of tea. She tried to soothe the new bride, and Clara answered her friend's pointed questions, not understanding where they were leading. Then Mrs. Kaplan smiled; she was sure she had discovered Clara's strange malady. Putting her arms around the distraught young woman, she looked at her.

"Clara, my *kynd*, you're not ill; I think you're going to have a baby!"

A startled Clara looked at her. "A baby?" She didn't believe it. "How could this happen?"

Clara, and most young women of her day, entered into marriage without any knowledge of the facts of life. A question of, "Where do babies come from?" was met with a look of absolute horror and an answer of: "Nice girls don't talk about such things!" If the question dared to be pursued by inquisitive young ladies, a mother would answer, "Iz kimt foon Gott [it comes from God]." Their questions of: "How?" were answered with: "When you get married you'll know."

To young people life remained a mystery—all to be solved on the wedding night and during married life!

Clara was so relieved she didn't have a serious illness but was so utterly bewildered and yet excited about the baby, she forgot about not feeling well. Her first thought was to run to the bakery and tell Usher, but she decided to go home, prepare dinner, and tell Usher that night.

She practically danced her way home, thrilled she was going to be a mother and Usher—a father!

After dinner, she couldn't wait to tell him her good news. It must have been a bolt out of the blue, as he didn't say anything. He just looked at her as if in shock, and then it finally seemed to register and he asked, surprised, "A baby?" He was totally unprepared for Clara's announcement.

Clara's spirits dampened somewhat. This wasn't the response she had anticipated. "Aren't you happy about the baby?"

Usher caught his second wind and hastened to reassure her, "Sure! Sure!" He knew there would be changes in their lives.

If ever there was a happy mother-to-be, it was Clara, and Usher seemed to be getting used to the idea. Clara shopped a few stores looking at baby things, then came home and sewed them for her baby. She took such enjoyment from every piece she made. Lovingly she folded them into a box, and every night she opened it and spread out her treasures, touching them softly. She couldn't wait for her child to be born.

Clara worked all summer and into the fall, but when winter came with the snow and cold, getting there became more of a problem. It was difficult getting up early while it was dark out and trying to make it through the snowdrifts to the streetcar. She knew the time was coming that she would have to stop working, and much as she disliked doing it, she did quit in the middle of December.

There were some things at home that troubled Clara. These were the arguments between Liz and her brother. They always began over little inconsequential things but soon developed into full-blown quarrels. One night, they became very angry with each other and Liz, in the heat of the argument, said she would find another place. Usher told her, "Go ahead." Neither one probably ever expected it to go this far, but it did.

Clara was more than upset with this turn of events. There had been many instances in the past when she tried to intervene, but if she said anything to one, the other got angry. Clara decided it best that she stay neutral and leave them to their seemingly senseless battles. She avoided the fights by going into the bedroom and shutting the door until the raving ceased.

Liz ran into her room crying, and Clara started after her. Usher, angry, told her to stay away, and she could see he was quite firm and meant it. That night she asked him to talk to Liz.

Clara couldn't sleep. Tired as she was, her thoughts were about Liz. What was she going to do?

The next morning Clara begged her not to leave. "He'll get over it. He didn't mean it," she pleaded. "Please, Liz, where will you go? Stay. I'll worry."

Both Usher and Liz were very obstinate and unchangeable, and neither would say, "I'm sorry." Those two little words, if said, would have changed many things that happened thereafter. Both were unyielding, and Liz left, leaving a heartbroken Clara.

With Liz gone and Clara unable to work, the couple couldn't keep the apartment. Usher had asked for a raise and was refused. "Who asks for a raise when things are not good in the shop?" Mr. Rosenbloom asked. Of course, this was a falsehood, and he knew it. Usher had worked for low wages for a long time and felt he should have gotten a little more compensation, even though things in general were not thriving.

Usher heard of another bakery, and did find another job with a little more pay. The drawback was that it was in Saint Paul, the city across the Mississippi River, only about ten miles away, but they would have to move. It was winter and Clara was against the move, but that didn't seem to make any difference to her husband. They moved.

Usher found a place, two rooms, and Clara made it into a home. This time it wasn't with much enthusiasm. The pregnancy made it difficult for her to move about. She was lonesome and resentful that Usher's temper had brought them to this situation. Her mind was deeply troubled.

On February 20, 1914, their daughter was born at home with the aid of a midwife. Clara named the child Slovie, after her beloved mother. Clara loved this child. She filled the huge void in Clara's life left by her missing family. She was confined to the small apartment the rest of the winter but didn't mind; she spent the time loving and nurturing her child.

Usher complained about the work, the hours, and his sleep, disturbed by the baby's crying. Clara tried her best to keep the child quiet, and when she couldn't, he flew into rages that frightened Clara.

They lived this way about a year; then Usher decided to go back to the Rosenbloom bakery. Clara didn't fight it; she was happy to get back to her friends.

Liz and Usher were not speaking to each other, and when Clara got back to Minneapolis, she took the baby to visit Liz. At first, the air was strained. In an accusatory tone Clara asked, "Why didn't you come to see me and the baby?"

Liz tried to justify her actions, "Because of Usher."

Liz held little Slovie while she and Clara talked of many things. Clara, crying softly, told of Usher's frequent outbursts of anger that she didn't understand. Liz wasn't too surprised.

Liz spoke of work and Sol. She was still seeing him.

"Any plans yet?"

Liz drew a deep sigh and shook her head. "No."

In America, the headlines screamed the news of an incident during a parade in Sarajevo, Bosnia, on June 28, 1914. The archduke Francis Ferdinand, heir to the throne of Austria, and his wife, Sophie, were assassinated.

Gavrilo Princep, who committed the act, was a member of a patriotic group of young Serbian students. They had been fighting to unite their people and free them from Austrian rule.

Europe had been threatened by war for a long time, and now Austria-Hungary blamed Serbia for the crime. Young Princep's murderous deed was the spark that set the smoldering nations aflame. A two-day ultimatum was sent to Serbia.

Austria's action was done with the backing of its allies, Germany and the German kaiser, Wilhelm II. Serbia began mobilizing its army, avoiding a direct reply. On July 2, Austria-Hungary declared war on Serbia.

Carol I of Romania died the year World War I began and was succeeded on the throne by Ferdinand, his nephew. Romania joined France, Great Britain, and their allies in the battle against the Central Powers—mainly Austria-Hungary and Germany. As the war went on, Italy, Greece, Japan, Portugal, and the United States joined the Allies. Then, later, Turkey and Bulgaria sided with Austria-Hungary and Germany.

To some Americans, this everyday news of events was ominous; to others, Europe was too far away from America and no concern for Americans.

To Clara, it was a concern; it involved her parents. Armies would soon be, if they weren't already, criss-crossing Romania. She knew what that meant, and it worried her. She had heard nothing from her parents and had tried unsuccessfully through organizations and other channels to contact them or get some word of them. It had been over two years.

Clara kept herself busy as all housewives and mothers do. She loved her little home and took pride in keeping it neat and clean. She cared for her child and did everything to please Usher. She visited her friends, and things were settling down to a somewhat normal state. Then Clara found she was pregnant again, and on October 15, 1915, "Tybel" (Tobie Nettie) was born.

That year the word from the war front was that Germany was using poisonous gas on the Russians, then against the French. After that gas was used on both sides. This worried, but still the Americans felt it wasn't here in America.

In 1915 a German U-boat sank the British passenger ship *Lusitania*, 124 Americans drowned, and this brought the United States to the brink of war.

Everyday life went on here. It wasn't easy trying to juggle the same amount of a paycheck for a growing family. Clara learned to stretch the food, making meals that cost little. Mrs. Kaplan taught her to cook, bake, pickle, and can. Clara had a natural knack for this; everything tasted wonderful.

Usher worked hard, and being tired was a perpetual state for him, both physically and mentally.

In America in 1916 President Wilson was reelected to a second term. He won on the campaign slogan: "He Kept Us Out of War."

On March 4, 1917, the Solomons were again visited by the stork and a third daughter, Raizel Gittel (Rose Gertrude), came into the world, a world being blown apart by the winds of war.

Germany's U-boats sank four American ships. Wilson called for a special session of Congress to ask for a declaration of war. War was declared against Germany on April 6, 1917.

Clara was only twenty-two years old, with a full Solomon household to care for. The children were beautiful, each with her own unique personality, and Clara adored them and spent her time caring for them, her husband, and their home. She enjoyed everything she did for them. Nothing was too much for her to do. She took her responsibilities seriously and was a devoted wife and mother.

Usher came home from the synagogue very excited these days. The men were discussing the war. The Selective Service Act passed on May 18, 1917. This act authorized the president to take the National Guard and the National Guard Reserve into federal service, but the president could also raise an additional military force by selective draft.

On July 5, about 9.5 million men between the ages of twenty-one and thirty-one registered. A few months later additional men between eighteen and forty-five were called up. This affected many homes in the north side community. This was a crisis many had not anticipated—Americans, their sons and husbands, having to go to war.

There were more important things to worry about besides making a living. The specter of war, and all the horrible things associated with it, hung over the community, in one way or another, and took people's minds off their old troubles and gave them new ones to concern themselves with.

It was this way for a while with Usher; then he went back to being his chronic complaining self, especially at home. His recurrent themes were his hard work, long hours, and constant irritation with his family. They were blamed for everything wrong in his life.

His temper was short-fused, and when it flared and an argument ensued, the children became frightened and cried. When he had succeeded in upsetting everyone, he went to bed, leaving Clara to soothe the youngsters until they quieted down.

She had thought she loved him. His handsome face, a cruel facade, had hidden his true selfish nature and vile temperament;

love had been blind, but she saw him now as he really was. Yet she found herself making excuses for him—he had never worked at a job in Romania and wasn't used to work—but in her heart she knew this wasn't so.

Many times she reminded him, "Here in America you have a trade, a job, a place to work. We're so lucky. Why aren't you satisfied? Happy?"

At times he complained of being ill and stayed home. His being ill worried her; she remembered her father's illness, when he couldn't work. She felt guilty and hovered over Usher, caring and nurturing to make him feel better.

Not going to work meant greatly reduced paychecks, and Clara had a trying time to make ends meet. No matter how she stretched the meager food supply, there was barely enough. She fed the children and Usher but many times did without herself, and the worry was taking its toll of her. No one knew about her problems except Mr. Rosenbloom. Clara kept them to herself.

Mrs. Kaplan noticed the change in her and became quite concerned. "I think you're working too hard, Clara."

One week when things were especially difficult, Clara stopped to pick up a little extra money owed her for a sweater she had made. The woman was very apologetic; she didn't have it. "Maybe next week," she said.

Clara mustered a weak smile. "That's all right."

She hurried away as tears stung her eyes, and the lump in her throat was so big, it just stuck there. She had planned on that bit of money for food. Quite disappointed, she went home to fix something. It was oatmeal again, but the youngsters didn't mind it. Clara always tried to make them happy. While they ate the mush again, she sang songs to them, songs she had heard her mother sing:

"Unter Raizeleh's viegeleh [under Rosie's little cradle]
Shtait a goldeneh tziegeleh [stands a tiny golden bird]."

Sometimes it was Slovie's name in the song, or Tobie's, and whichever child it was would smile and listen. It was something special for that child alone.

Sometimes they joined in singing with her. Soon they were laughing, happy to be together, Clara and her children.

Quarrels with her husband became frequent. Clara a very private, proud person, knew the neighbors heard them. She was embarrassed and ashamed. *How can I walk out on the street the next day? How can I hold my head up?* she thought.

There was a change in Clara, from a bubbly, vivacious person with a great sense of humor to a very subdued, quiet one.

Mrs. Kaplan, who loved this young woman as one of her own, saw many disturbing signs of unhappiness. Laughter didn't come as easily anymore, and when Clara tried to smile, her eyes were sad, as if life had gone from them. She didn't come as often when she was invited, always making excuses.

So many times Clara wanted to visit Mrs. Kaplan, to speak with her. She felt the need to unburden her heart, but how could she confide her problems with Usher to anyone? This was a family affair, and that would have been a betrayal! She couldn't do it!

Mrs. Kaplan, too, had thought about speaking to Clara, but knowing Clara's feelings about privacy, she had to respect Clara's silence, while admiring the young woman's strengths. She agonized, nevertheless, as she watched a troubled Clara's efforts to weather the storms in her marriage.

At night while Usher slept beside her, Clara lay awake there, motionless, staring into the nothingness. Pondering serious questions of herself, she wondered what she could do about this situation. She couldn't control his vile temper—the slightest thing would set it off—and she couldn't change his selfishness. His concerns were always about himself.

Clara tried to discuss matters with him, but he wouldn't answer. When he did, it was always with an argument.

Usher left early one morning. That night Clara nervously waited dinner for him. She stood at the window and wondered, *Where can he be?*

She spent a wakeful, restless night—up at every sound—worried something had happened to him.

The next morning, opening the closet door, she discovered his clothes missing. The old suitcase was gone, too. When and where had he taken them? Her heart pounding, she ran to the bakery.

Usher had taken his pay and left the day before. "Where are you going?" Mr. Rosenbloom had asked him when he saw his suitcase.

Mr. Rosenbloom, visibly shaken, didn't relish imparting this information to Clara. From Mr. Rosenbloom Clara learned that Usher had regularly received mail from New York.

"From New York?" She looked at Mr. Rosenbloom as she tried to fully comprehend what the man was saying. None of it made any sense to her. Who was he writing to in New York that it had been kept secret? Could this account for the behavior she had been unable to understand? She didn't know him at all. She wrung her hands, completely devastated. *How could Usher do this to me and the children? How could he?* she wondered.

She went back slowly to the children, alone at home. She went to their beds and looked down at them sleeping. Tears streamed down her face. Gently she touched each child's head. They slept undisturbed, unaware of what was happening to their world and the difference it would make in their lives. The baby was only six months old.

Clara didn't even undress and went to bed with sobs racking her body. She covered her mouth with both hands so her crying wouldn't waken the children. Later, much later, she closed her eyes and flashbacks of their life together whirled in her brain. They came quickly and just as quickly changed, like pictures in a kaleidoscope. There were the happy days growing up in Romania, the picture of his welcoming glance when he met her on her arrival in Minneapolis. She seemed to calm down, remembering the dating when she lived at the Kaplans', the picture of their wedding, and their first home. These were days of wonderful memories.

Then it began to change. There were the numerous quarrels with Liz and the job changes. Suddenly the pictures were turning ugly; arguments and bad temper.

Everything had happened gradually and she didn't see where it was all leading. Now, she opened her eyes and lay there, not feeling anything, just numbness.

She became angry, angry with herself. She tortured herself with questions of *Was I to blame? What could I have done differently? Could I have stopped it before it got to the "point of no return"?*

She thought about the arguments between brother and sister in Romania. They were frequent, about so many things. Clara had not put too much portent to them. It hadn't concerned her. Was this her mistake? For the questions that now tormented her she had no answers.

She didn't know how she was going to make it through the next day, or the day after that. He had gone, leaving her without money. She went to speak to the landlady and explain her situation. She would be late with the rent. She worried, *What if I have to move again?*

The landlady was quite understanding. "I can wait for a few weeks, Clara. Don't worry." She had heard the quarrels and his constant complaints and seen his temper displayed so many times.

She had wondered how the young woman could deal with it day after day.

Clara couldn't afford to feel sorry for herself; there was much to do. She hurried to the sign maker's shop, and the next morning, there hung the sign: "Dressmaker Upstairs," and Clara started her business. She thought of Gittel and her persistence to make Clara learn the different sewing techniques. *Thank God I listened,* Clara thought now.

She hoped people would come to her. She would always do her best; she knew that. Her confidence was mixed with fear and uncertainty, but she was a woman of quiet courage and took on the challenge as breadwinner for her family.

The first week brought a few customers. Clara took care of the children during the day and did her sewing at night after they were put to bed. Every night but Friday night, the Sabbath, she sewed until three or four o'clock in the morning. Word of mouth from satisfied customers brought her some new ones. She earned barely enough to get by, but she never complained. *Thank God I can work at home and care for my children,* she thought. As always, they were her main concern.

Usher had been gone for over a year. Clara heard he was in New York working at a bakery shop there. She had no word from him. Friends spoke to her about obtaining a divorce. She had never heard of divorce, and they tried to explain it to her. What she understood about it made her sad. "I know," she said, "it's not a good thing."

Very early one morning Mr. Rosenbloom came to open the shop and was surprised to find Usher standing there. He wanted Mr. Rosenbloom to intercede, on his behalf, with Clara. He wanted Clara to take him back.

"I want to go back to her. I'll be different," he begged.

Mr. Rosenbloom became quite upset. "Go see her yourself."

His heart pounded as he watched the young man leave to see his wife. He knew all the trouble the young woman had been through. Everybody knew her as a wonderful young woman.

In his heart, the baker prayed, *Don't let her take him back. She would be making a big mistake!*

Usher's hand trembled as he knocked on the door. He could hear the children as they played together. Clara opened the door, shocked and surprised when she saw him. Her first thought was to shut the door. She felt anger rising up within her.

"Voos vilst du daw? [What do you want here?]" she wanted to know.

"I want to come back."

"You want to come back? You never sent a word to me or anything for the children. How could you do this to us? What were you thinking?"

"I'm sorry," he mumbled low, so low she could hardly hear him.

She looked at him. All kinds of feelings welled up in her. She took a deep breath. "No." She shook her head sadly. "Usher, we can't live together again."

She stood aside when he tried to speak with the two older children, but they wouldn't come to him.

"Where are you staying?" She thought it was with Lizzie, but it wasn't. They were still not talking to each other.

Clara thought about it, but she didn't invite him in. They had nothing to say to each other.

He turned to leave and she shut the door. Standing there with her back against the door and her hand still on the doorknob, she shut her eyes and heaved a deep sigh of pain. Moments later she walked to the window and saw him moving down the street, out of their lives once again.

Clara served Usher with divorce papers. She had given it much thought, all they had been through, the children and, yes, Usher, too! It wasn't an easy thing to do, but it was necessary to close that chapter of their lives. Usher went back to New York. Clara lived with hope that tomorrow would be better.

In 1919 Clara received her divorce in the American court. Evidently there were sufficient grounds. Whatever they were, she never talked about them.

This had been a difficult thing for her to go through. She was heartbroken and disillusioned. In a divorce, no one wins. Everyone loses!

But with all her heartaches, she learned to smile again. "The one thing good to come out of that marriage was my children," she said often.

The year Clara got her divorce, Liz and Sol were finally married. Clara was not invited to the wedding. Liz, still not on speaking terms with her brother, nevertheless was angry with Clara because she had refused to let Usher come back and had divorced him. Sol, who had always been on good terms with Clara and sided with her, wanted Clara at the wedding but couldn't start his wedding with an argument, so had to accede to Liz's wishes.

Clara, after the divorce, never talked about Usher or answered questions about him. She never even mentioned his name. She would say, "It's enough I had to go through it." She would never discuss "it," and the "it" was left that way—unanswered questions.

The day the divorce was final Clara took down the wedding picture in the living room and had Usher taken out of it. The picture was hung back on the wall—a picture of a beautiful bride, young and vulnerable, standing there alone.

So many times Clara looked at the picture. What thoughts did it evoke? It blocked out the few happy memories, and what was left was bitter. She had made a mistake. She learned when we make mistakes, knowingly or unwittingly, we pay a price. The price for Clara and her children was incalculable!

Part III

Clara's Family

Chapter 24

"Because You're the Oldest!"

Although the Armistice had been signed on November 11, 1918, more than a year before, and the war was ended, the country now was engulfed in the struggle to find its way out of the turmoil—abroad and especially at home. The terrible war had cost the United States over $20 billion, not including the loans to the Allies. The tally of suffering totaled more than fifty thousand deaths and two hundred thousand men wounded.

Everyone was hysterically happy as they welcomed the heroes home, but the men returned to find their country in the throes of its long postwar depression years.

Families in the community, like families around the country, found themselves without jobs, and money was a scarce commodity.

People who had always lived with hard times and frustration and fear now found themselves in worsening adverse circumstances. The need and worry were there in their faces and in their eyes.

With almost everyone in this calamitous predicament, it wasn't any wonder that Clara found fewer customers in need of her sewing skills! Her livelihood depended on her own two hands. Sewing was all she knew how to do. She had struggled before, and it had been barely sufficient to help with her family responsibilities, but it had been a living.

What had been most important to her was the fact that she could work at home and care for her children, too. Clara had to find new ways to face her problems, and time was of the essence. What could she do to bring in that extra dollar or so she needed so desperately? She had to find new ways to face her problems.

Many times her children were awakened by the monotonous sound, the up and down of the treadle on the sewing machine, as she pedaled miles into the night—sewing, sewing, sewing.

She created different things she liked personally and hoped other women would like them and find a need for them, for themselves or as gifts for family members or friends.

Clara hurried through the early mornings getting the children ready, then put the wares in the baby carriage with the youngest child. The other two came along with her, one on each side, as she walked them to school. They said their good-byes with hugs and kisses, and off they went, their different ways.

Then Clara began her trudging from house to house, first in one neighborhood, then another, always optimistic. *Today will be a good day!* she told herself.

She soon found it wasn't an easy task knocking on doors, standing there waiting, wondering who would open the door and how receptive they would be. Clara was turned away many times, and discouragement crept in, to mix with the optimism as the morning wore on.

Being a woman, she knew women were shoppers, and many did come out to look. Often the story was the same: very little money to spend. Clara could see they really were interested and wanted her things. Why shouldn't they have them?

She was an entrepreneur, way ahead of her time. She manufactured her items and was the salesperson extolling their benefits. She was running her own little business and now started her own line of credit.

"If you want it, take it," she would say when she saw them lingering over some of the articles. "You can pay me later," she coaxed, but never pressured. Clara trusted them and they knew her to be a woman of integrity, always trying to satisfy them. Many times she sewed all night to fill an order for someone who needed it the next day. She never asked for payment and knew when they had it they would give it to her.

It all was working out wonderfully well, and she was pleased to have found this way out of her predicament. She was thankful and voiced this sentiment out loud. "Ah, dahnken, Gott!" She clasped her hands together and looked up at the sky as if she could see Him when she talked to Him!

The weeks and months flew and life was, more or less, on an even keel, of course with its inevitable ups and downs, but she could pay her rent, had food for the children, and they were together—a family!

But, somehow, it wasn't meant for things to go along smoothly for too long a stretch of time. There were always interruptions of some sort or other, upsetting the scheme of things, and so it was when, tragically, Clara began to experience trouble with her eyes.

It started in small ways, unnoticeable at first—slight headaches and then blurring vision. It got progressively worse, and soon she was unable to sew or fill even the smallest order. Clara hadn't complained; she was sure it would go away. But it didn't.

Her dear friend Mrs. Kaplan had noticed and tried to get her to go to a doctor. Foolishly Clara delayed getting any help, which greatly concerned her friends. As the days passed she knew it was serious and went to an eye clinic.

When she came home, she was terribly upset, and justifiably so—the doctors told her surgery was necessary, with a stay in the hospital, and they recommended it be soon.

All night she worried how it could be done. How could she go? What could she do about her children? These questions tormented her.

"Clara, you must go. Your situation will only get worse," Mrs. Kaplan begged her.

"My children! My children!" Clara's stress was in her voice and visible in her face.

"We will take care of the children. Don't worry," her friends told her.

The days were hectic as Clara made preparations to leave. She was filled with fear for herself, going through this surgery. The fear was mostly the worry and concern for her children, having to leave them. She had never imagined that she would be ill, unable to care for them. Outwardly, she tried to be brave for them. It was enough for them to be separated from her.

The next morning, the youngest child went to Mrs. Kaplan's and Slovie and Tobie to other neighbors. From the first anguish-filled night they missed Clara. What if something happened to her? Where would they go? Would they be separated from each other forever?

They felt so alone in a world that seemed so big. Tobie cried, wanting to be with Slovie, and Slovie cried, wanting to be with Tobie and the baby. If they could just be together, things wouldn't seem so bad. They were told they couldn't be together but the children couldn't comprehend that three of them together were too much for strangers to take care of. They knew their mother did it.

Their little faces were sad and they didn't smile, couldn't smile, even though the people they were with were kind. The experience of not seeing their mother or each other was an agonizing one. They questioned constantly, tearfully, "When is my mom coming back?"

Good neighbors, well meaning, failed to understand the trauma of the children and answered them vaguely, causing them further anxiety.

In the minds of the children, they were sure they would never see their mother or each other again. The days passed slowly and were endlessly long.

Slovie, consumed with fear for her mother, didn't know for sure who it was she spoke to in the darkness of the room one night. She thought it was God. Hadn't her mother told her, "God is everywhere!"? Slovie promised, with all the earnestness of a child, "I'll be good and do whatever Mom wants if You will only make her better." Tears started. "Please make her better so she can come home."

It was a promise, a pact, Slovie made with God, and she would try to keep it.

After what seemed like an eternity, Clara came home, and the children were happy to be home and together. The experiences of the past week had been difficult for them, and they were quite noticeably subdued.

Their mother had to rest quietly, and it was frightening to see her with her eyes bandaged, speaking to them in a weakened voice, and not seeing them, but they stayed in the room to be with her.

Clara had to depend on Slovie for many things during this period of recuperation. The youngster never complained but went willingly—thankful in her heart God had made it possible for her mother to be home. He had answered her prayer, so Slovie was fulfilling her part of the "promise."

She learned to help with the younger sisters, too, and her mother called her Mamaleh.

At last the bandages came off, to everyone's relief. Clara still suffered pain and sought help from numerous doctors. The surgery, she learned, was unsuccessful and only worsened her condition. Her caring friends were most helpful, but they had their own families to look after. Clara was thankful to have them; just knowing that made her feel better.

The doctors were emphatic about one thing—she would have to quit sewing and take the strain from her eyes or face the possibility of blindness, a real possibility!

Clara knew she would have to seek other means of employment, knowing full well any kind would take her from her children. It was worrisome and difficult for her to accept that eventually they would be spending time home alone. One consolation to her was knowing, as she said, "My children are good children."

She had to find a job soon. In desperation she finally accepted the one that had the least obstacles. Its main drawback was that she had to move to Saint Paul again. It was low-paying, as most were, and was in a meat-packing plant in South Saint Paul that employed mostly immigrant women. So many times Clara spoke about the new job, about the problems that were daily occurrences. Clara and the other women worked in a large, very cold, damp room. The floors were always wet, and the women wore rubbers and stood on wooden planks, raised one inch off the floor. The damp cold penetrated deep into every bone of their bodies.

Their job was stuffing sausage skins as fast as they could. They were paid by the hour, but quotas for the hour had to be met. Working conditions were deplorable, but there were no complaints. With the scarcity of jobs and hundreds lined up for every one available, a person considered himself fortunate to have one of any kind.

The women had to pay for their white uniforms and were required to wear a fresh one every day. Clara could only afford one, so it had to be laundered and ironed every night.

Often unwelcome breezes carried the offensive, revolting odors from the meat-packing plant, saturating the neighborhood air. Housewives hurried to quickly close the windows, even on the warmest days. People held their noses and walked around with headaches. Trying to cook was difficult; trying to eat was worse. It was an intolerable situation for the women working there. Clara often came home so nauseous she couldn't eat. She had been inhaling the foul stench all day, which was unbearable and made her ill.

By six-thirty every morning, Clara had already dressed, fed, and deposited her youngest child, Rosie, at the neighbor's across the street. Slovie and Tobie stayed upstairs in the one room that was now their home. Clara paid the landlady to watch her children, but she didn't do a very good job and they were mostly left alone. Clara, suspecting this, delegated the duty of caring for Tobie to Slovie. "I know you will take good care of her for me, Slovie."

Only once Slovie rebelled and questioned, "Why me, Mom?"

"Why?" Clara said. "Because you're the oldest!" According to Clara, that put Slovie in a special category, which carried with it certain obligations to the family. Slovie became caretaker and protector and grew up with that commitment to her siblings.

They played outdoors on warm summer days, sometimes until Clara came home from work. The cold winters created other problems, since they had to stay in the one room. Needless to say, tempers flared as the siblings quarreled and cried, which brought the landlady's broom pounding on the ceiling for them to be quiet.

125

Many times, Tobie wouldn't calm down, which brought the landlady stomping up the stairs, scolding, shaking her finger as she angrily reprimanded them, "I will tell your mama!" Then down she went, muttering to herself, "Ah zoineh kinder! [Such children!]" Clara's children were just average normal youngsters. The landlady just didn't like kids. Sometimes when they grew tired and came to sit on the porch for a while, she came out and chased them away. They couldn't sit on the sidewalk in front of the house, so they played around the corner. Upstairs in their room they walked barefoot or in stockings across the floor so as to keep the noise level down.

The children knew it upset Clara when the landlady complained about them. Clara worried she would have to move, and it wouldn't be easy to find another place. She couldn't pay more rent.

The children, naturally, missed their mother. Tobie kept calling for her and usually began to cry when she couldn't do as she wanted. Slovie felt she was letting her mom down if she couldn't keep her sister happy. So many times Slovie wished her mom could be home with them. They learned life just wasn't perfect!

The one room they lived in was not very large. Rosie, the three-year-old, slept in an iron crib off to one corner. Slovie and Tobie slept with their mother in a bed certainly not built for three. The children, tired out from the day's activities, usually fell asleep and slept peacefully, but other times their restlessness kept Clara awake.

There was a two-burner gas plate that stood on a small stand in front of a curtained window. Twice the curtain caught fire, causing worry to Clara, excitement for the children and neighborhood when the firemen arrived, and great consternation to the landlady, who threatened to evict them if it happened again. Clara took the curtain down!

They shared the bathroom down the hall with the grown-ups from downstairs, and it seemed to the children that the bathroom was always in use when they needed it, but the adults grumbled that the children were always in it. They pounded on the door, shouting, "Arois! Arois! [Out! Out!]"

The children also remembered many wonderful childhood experiences as they were growing up. Baths were taken in a large, round galvanized tub that Clara used for washing their clothes. The girls watched as their mother heated water in the teakettle and one large pot. They took their baths, splashing water at each other while puddles formed on the floor. They kept Clara busy mopping up the water so it wouldn't drip downstairs. They laughed, like children

126

without cares, but Clara had to remind them not to be too noisy. She would put her finger to her lips, "Sh! Sh!"; then she'd point downstairs. They'd all giggle with fingers to their mouths, "Sh! Sh!"

In summer when the weather was hot, it was a task to get them out. No one wanted to leave the cool refreshing water. The winter was quite another story. They shivered, covered with goose bumps, teeth chattering, lips blue, as they washed up quickly to see who could get out first and jump into the bed Clara had made warm with a hot water bottle. They snuggled—life was good!

The quick wash-up left much to be desired. Clara checked their ears and feet and groaned. "Oy vey! [Oh, dear!]" She kissed them anyway, so they knew she loved them, clean or dirty!

On cold, wintry, or rainy days, the children stayed indoors. It was Slovie's job to keep her sister busy and happy, and it wasn't easy. If she didn't get her way, she cried.

Usually, it was a learning time, the eldest teaching the younger one. Slovie taught Tobie to count, to tell time, and the colors of crayons, and they cut tons of old paper into paper dolls, making dresses and hats as Clara had shown them. They kept themselves busy. When at last they heard the welcome sound of their mother coming up the stairs, out they jumped, leaving the mess to be cleaned up later.

They met Clara with a bombardment of complaints. Tobie (who couldn't say "Slovie") would enumerate all the things "Suie" would not let her do or have, while Clara tried to settle Rosie down. ("Suie" later became "Sue," and as Slovie grew up, everyone called her Sue except her mother.) Slovie had only followed her mother's instructions and felt she was doing a good job.

Next the landlady came up complaining. Clara, tired, listened to her patiently, not saying a word. She didn't want to antagonize the landlady any further. Clara promised her children would do better.

After the landlady left, Clara sat on the bed, head bent, and the children knew she was crying. Slovie always felt bad, as if she had created this situation, as if she were somehow to blame by not doing a good-enough job caring for her sister.

Her thoughts would vacillate, knowing she had done as her mom had asked and aware at the same time of her sister's obstinacy in refusing to cooperate and the problems that followed. Slovie was sure it was because Tobie was younger, and in time she would learn.

The next morning, when Clara was leaving, she said, "Let Tobie do what she wants, so she won't cry." Tobie learned to take advantage of this in manipulating ways.

The children being home with a landlady who was constantly scolding them gave Clara very little peace at work. All day she worried; they were alone. At the end of the day's work, when she hurried up the stairs, they ran, happy to see her. What they didn't know was how thankful she was to see them safe and together.

In their one room they had a dresser with an oval mirror. Clara kept it covered with a lace scarf. On one side, she kept a brush and comb, and on the other, a cup half-filled with water that held a few yellow dwarf marigolds from the yard downstairs. Sometimes in summer there were a few bright blue morning glories, and every few days there were new fresh flowers in the little cup, which Clara arranged ever so carefully. They were a most pleasurable sight. Clara's face would brighten as she set the flower-filled cup down on the dresser. "These remind me of the beautiful flowers we had home in Romania," she would say. She would turn thoughtful at the good memory and smile.

The younger ones were asleep. Slovie begged her mother, "Tell me a story about home, Mom."

Clara thought awhile, and as Slovie snuggled close, she began. Slovie listened with delight. She never tired of hearing her mother's stories. And there were many—stories of life in Romania that her father had told her and stories she told of when she was young. Her stories spoke to Slovie's imagination and so enriched her life.

Flowers in the cup were Slovie's first recollection of pretty fresh flowers in their home. As hard as life was for them, their mother, in so many ways, managed to bring something special—little things, but beautiful, into their lives. This time it was not only the love of nature—flowers—but of stories of her life!

Clara's days were long and she was often quite tired, but on Friday night the children were cleaned up and ready for the Sabbath. It was the one day they ate together.

Clara set the small narrow bench that served as a table, and they sat crowded, bright-eyed, and full of expectation as they watched her light the *Shabbos* candles, then chant the prayer. She would smile at them and say, "*Goot Shabbos, kinderlach* [good Sabbath, children]," and they answered, "*Goot Shabbos,* Mom!"

Sometimes when she finished the prayer, they saw her wipe away a tear. They hated to see her unhappy. "Why are you crying, Mom?"

"Why? Why?" She raised her hands heavenward. "*Shabbos* is

so beautiful. It reminds me of happy times with my parents and little brother. God should only watch over them, wherever they are." This was a prayer she voiced many times. Her family was far away across the sea, but they were never far from her—always in her heart. She was always concerned for their safety.

Clara served the special Friday night dinner she had prepared the night before and kept in the icebox downstairs. Once a week, she paid ten cents for her share of the ice for the box.

"Mom, can I have a chicken wing?"

They all loved chicken wings, and soon all were clamoring for what to them was a delicacy. But a chicken had only two wings.

"I asked first," a sibling would whine. Then another would begin and a ruckus would start, but Clara quieted them down with, "Kinderlach, it's *Shabbos*. No fighting."

She began to ladle out the soup, and everyone received a wonderfully plump chicken wing. The children squealed with delight and were surprised the first time this happened.

"Mom, how come there are so many wings on this chicken?"

Clara had a wonderful sense of humor. She looked at them and answered, "These are special chickens with three wings God makes for *Shabbos*, because *Shabbos* is so special."

Her children believed it for a long time. Young as they were, they learned how special *Shabbos* and holidays were, and it was the beginning of love for their heritage and traditions.

Years later the children learned every Friday their mother exchanged a chicken leg for a chicken wing with the landlady downstairs and that was how they had the three-winged chicken for *Shabbos!*

The children missed their mother not being home like other mothers but knew she had no choice, so it was accepted. However, Clara didn't work on Saturdays or Sundays. How wonderful it was for her children to go out to play and come home calling, "Mom! Mom!" They saw her standing at the top of the stairs with her wonderful welcoming smile. What an incredible feeling that was— their mother was home, and for a little while all was well with their world!

Chapter 25

Bad Times and Good

Sometimes, on Sunday, the family was invited to the home of one of Clara's new friends. They always had fun visiting, racing outdoors and through the house with abandon. Clara would scold, reminding the children to behave.

While the youngsters played, the women sat in the kitchen catching up on events of the week. They listened as Clara told stories of the people she worked with and happenings on the job. They became so interested, she had to continue when they met again, like a miniseries. Clara brought a new dimension to their lives—she was the only mother working and making her own living. They had great respect for her, but she knew they didn't understand how hard it was.

The women prepared meals together while they talked and laughed and shared confidences. Clara always brought her share, usually something everyone liked. Slovie heard them complimenting her mother, "Clara, everything has such *tom.*" Clara did have a wonderful natural talent for cooking and baking. Four women could make the same recipe, but somehow, Clara's was always tastier! No one could make knishes, strudel, pickles, and other mouthwatering delicacies as tasty as Clara's.

Slovie didn't know when it was she became aware that her family was different from others. She noticed there was a man in the homes of her mother's friends. He was "Pa" to the children, their father.

The night of her discovery, she asked her mom, "Why don't we have a father?"

Clara had not expected that question from her child. Parents always assume the child is too young and there is time in the future to discuss situations. A little shocked, she was silent for a long time; then she answered, but her voice and manner had become tense. "You have a father. He just doesn't live with us."

"Why?"

"We're divorced."

"What does that mean, divorced?"

"You're too young to understand, and I don't want to talk about it."

"Where is he?" Slovie's questions continued.

"I don't know, and don't ask me." Then Clara began to cry.

For a long time Slovie didn't ask again. She just wondered and thought about it a great deal. She didn't like being different and wished she had a father.

Enviously she watched a friend hop-skip alongside her father as they went to the store. Slovie got so angry, she bounced her ball hard against the screen door, back and forth, until the landlady came out yelling. But the bouncing ball had done its job of therapy, and Slovie's anger had subsided.

When the family came home from their Sunday visits, Clara was always happier. Her spirits were uplifted, as if being with her friends had pumped new life, new energy, into her being. She was ready to take on the coming week with all its trials and tribulations of hard, monotonous work and the constant worry and caring for her "beautiful children," as she called them.

When Slovie looked back and remembered this time, she thought each day for her mom must have seemed like an eternity. The children saw her smile and cry, tired, and in her heart there must have been many sad, lonely times and concern for what was to be.

Clara worried when the children became ill. Slovie and Tobie caught the mumps, and when Rosie came down with scarlet fever they were quarantined, with a big, ugly yellow sign from the Health Department nailed on the front door. Slovie was angry with Rosie because she had to stay out of school for thirty days. Then she was very remorseful and was sure God would punish her because she had been selfish, thinking of herself and not worrying about her little sister, who then reaped the benefit of extra attention!

Then Tobie and Slovie caught the measles. Their room was darkened with a blanket hung over the window. They were in for almost a week and told not to move the blanket or look out. There they were like prisoners, not feeling well, and crabby with each other. Poor Clara, she stayed home for two days with them.

When Clara went to the store, Tobie moved the blanket aside to look out and would not let Slovie see. Slovie went downstairs and out into the sunshine. She didn't see her mother coming from the landlady's house.

"What are you doing down here? Oy vey tzi mere! [Oh, woe is me!] You're going to go blind!"

Slovie ran upstairs, her mom following. Tobie was looking out the window talking to a friend and hadn't heard them coming, so she was caught, too. She received her share of the scolding. Both girls began to cry. They had never seen their mother so angry with them.

Her children were her everything, and now their disobedience had given her a new worry. She was sure looking out at the daylight, being in the sun, would cause them to go blind.

They didn't go near the blanketed window again. Every morning, Slovie opened her eyes and then would call to her mother with the good news, "Mom, I can still see!"

She'd answer, "Ah, dahnken Gott!"

When they became ill with other things, their mom knew exactly what to do. She could have hung out her shingle: "Dr. Mom"! She had more remedies that worked. Sore throats were treated with a concoction of hot milk, melted butter, and honey. The children put up a fight and tried to refuse it even though, later, they had to admit it was soothing and didn't taste bad at all. Stiff necks were rubbed with Vick's Vapo Rub and covered with a piece of flannel. Vick's was Clara's wonder drug—she rubbed it on their chests if they had coughs, and into their noses if they were stuffy or had the sniffles!

They had their share of colds, but not too many, because their mother made little drawstring fabric bags, about two inches by three inches. They were filled with camphor crystals that were strong-smelling and hung around the girls' necks with a red string. Clara was sure they kept colds away. The red string was supposed to protect her "beautiful children" from anyone's "evil eye." Clara was a little superstitious!

The children kept Clara busy with their banged heads and cut fingers. They couldn't afford to wear shoes in the summer but didn't know that was why they went barefoot. They thought it was another wonderful thing their mother let them do. So every day one of them came home crying, with cut toes or heels from the broken glass in the street where they played.

Their scratched and bruised elbows and knees miraculously healed when their mom took care of them. Her patience was inexhaustible! She exuded confidence and strength as she accepted the challenge of every problem the children brought to her. They grew up seeing this strong, capable woman who was warm and nurturing. To their minds, she could do anything, and to all of them she was everything!

The July Fourth weekend was coming up. Usually they stayed home watching other children shoot firecrackers or burn "sparklers," but Clara told them they were going to Como Park with another family. They were traveling on the streetcar, and they were going to have a picnic. For days the girls talked of nothing else, they were so excited. These were all new experiences they were looking forward to with such anticipation.

"This is a special Fourth of July," Clara told her children. "It's the first since the war ended."

When the day finally arrived, they rushed their mother from the time they woke up. They were the most impatient youngsters and bothered Clara repeatedly with their questions of, "What time are we going to go?" "Is it time yet?" "Are you ready, Mom?"

Their mom just quit answering the endless questions, so they had to go downstairs and wait. Seconds seemed like hours, so they took turns running up to see how things were coming along. Of course the landlady came out to give her voice its daily exercise by scolding the children for opening the screen door so many times.

Clara put their lunch in the straw suitcase. Curious, Slovie asked, "What are we going to have?"

"It's a surprise. You'll see when we get there."

Their mother loved surprises. The children tingled with excitement and couldn't wait. It was something nice to look forward to, and they were never disappointed.

At last they seemed to be ready, but then their mother called out, "Better go to the bathroom, everybody!" They scampered like jackrabbits to perform this last bit of important business before they set off.

Clara gave Slovie the jar of lemonade to carry. She clutched the bag it was in, but it kept slipping. She worried, *What if I drop it? That would certainly be a calamity. What would we drink?*

With great determination, she grasped the bag more tightly. She would get the lemonade there, because she took any duty very seriously.

Clara took the baby, Rosie, in one arm, and the suitcase in the other, and off they started.

"Take Slovie's hand," Clara ordered Tobie.

Slovie interjected, "Mom, I can't take her hand and hold the jar. I might drop it!"

"All right." Clara looked at Tobie, who was pouting. "Hold onto Slovie's dress then."

This settled, the travelers set off.

They walked slowly to the car line a few blocks away—Clara, her arms full, and Slovie, trying to juggle the jar of lemonade, with Tobie holding her back, tugging on her dress.

For the children, the ride on the streetcar took forever. They began to pester, "When are we going to get there?"

"It's not too far now," Clara assured them.

They rode a few more blocks and asked, "Are we going to be there pretty soon?"

Clara tried to quiet them, as the "little one" had fallen asleep.

They reached their destination not too long after that. The streetcar clanged as people were carelessly crossing the car tracks; then it came to a halt and they got off into the crowds.

Clara headed for the pavilion and found the other family, the wife and her two children. The husband couldn't come. Clara and her friend walked together; the children ran on in front of them, staying close so as not to get lost in the huge crowd. Every once in a while Clara stopped to count heads.

The ladies found a spot they both agreed on. It was on a hill, under a tree to shade them from the sun that was beginning to climb higher in the sky. From this spot they could see the pavilion, the grandstand, and the lake where the fireworks would take place later. It was a perfect spot!

The children soon played tag and hide-go-seek while the mothers relaxed and got caught up on things important to them, Then, as expected, began the clamoring for food.

The chorus of young voices began, "Mom, we're thirsty!" Next it was, "When do we eat?"

Clara spread out a tablecloth, and the children knelt down and watched as she poured the lemonade into tin cups. They squealed with delight as their mother handed them their favorite kosher salami sandwiches, which tasted even better with her pickles. With great relish, they wolfed the sandwiches down. The sandwiches had never tasted so good, perhaps because this was taking place "in the great outdoors," in the fresh air.

Clara wanted them to rest on the blanket for a while, so they lay down, looking up at a blue sky and trees.

"Look." Clara pointed out a nest not too high up in a tree. They could see two birds. "See the mother and father birds feeding the little baby birds," she said softly.

They watched, entranced. "Oh, yes, we see them!"

"Oy!" she said. "A miracle from God!"

Through their mother they learned of God's love for all His creatures and grew up caring about them.

After they had rested, Clara gave them each a penny to get their treat, a small ice-cream cone. They hopped and skipped along to the pavilion and took their places at the end of a very long line. They bubbled over with excitement. They loved ice cream. Today it was their mom's special treat, "a surprise!"

Slovie checked with her younger sisters. "Where is your money?"

They opened their small perspiring hands that had been clenched tightly over their pennies, then shut them quickly for fear of losing the coins.

Little by little they inched up in the long line, then gave the white-aproned, white-capped lad behind the counter the money as he put the precious chocolate ice-cream cones into each of their outstretched hands. Now, the treat was really theirs! They stepped aside and licked the tops that were beginning to drip, savoring every taste.

Slovie took Tobie's hand and she took Rosie's and they started back down the crowded stairs and sidewalk to their mom. They saw her standing looking for them. It had taken so long she had become quite anxious, but Slovie explained about the long line.

"Mom, I knew we were all right." Slovie said it matter-of-factly. "We were all together."

"I know, Sloveleh. Next time I won't worry," she said, "because they're with you." She patted Slovie's head gently and looked at her in her special way, always eye to eye.

The band was beginning to gather on the bandstand, and they could hear the different instruments tuning up. The lights came on, and the director took his place on the podium. Then the band struck up wonderful, stirring music. One song stayed in Slovie's mind. It was a toe-tapping, rousing piece. She learned it was "Stars and Stripes Forever."

They watched the fireworks explode that evening. As each one shot up into the dark sky, beautiful showers of colored stars burst forth, and everyone heard the "ohs" and "ahs" of appreciation of this breathtaking spectacle.

"Look here, Mom!" One pointed in one direction. "Mom, Mom, look over there!" The other pointed in the opposite direction. Each wanted her mother to see what she was discovering. Clara's head swung back and forth like the pendulum on a clock, but somehow she kept them all happy.

When it was time to go, tired as they were, they didn't want to leave—they didn't want it to end! They had never been out so late, which was another wonderful experience for them.

Clara carried the "little one," who was asleep, and the others followed her onto the waiting streetcar. This had indeed been a most memorable day. They were all keyed up with the excitement of it when they arrived home, straggling after their mother.

Getting ready for bed, Slovie wanted to know, "Why do we celebrate Fourth of July, Mom?"

Her mother's voice spoke with strong emotion. "It's America's birthday of freedom. We should never forget it, Sloveleh. We are lucky to be here."

She had told many stories of the oppression of Jews and of her family in Romania, how her parents had wanted her to be free of anti-Semitism, so she had come here, leaving them behind. Clara's children had not yet encountered anti-Semitism and couldn't fully understand it.

America had accepted Clara, given her freedom. She wanted to give something back. For now, all she could do was be a law-abiding citizen.

"Someday," Clara said, "I hope I have a home so I can hang out the American flag on the Fourth of July to celebrate the birthday of this Golden Land." It was a wish she hoped to fulfill.

Clara made the children understand what freedom meant to her. She taught them patriotism. They all grew up respecting and loving their country.

It was late. Clara kissed them all good night. The baby was asleep.

"Schloof, kinderlach [sleep, children]."

They snuggled in, feeling safe and loved.

Always after that, whenever Slovie heard "Stars and Stripes Forever" a bounty of warm memories would come to mind. She could close her eyes and see it all again. She could almost taste the goodness of those salami sandwiches, see the troublesome jar of lemonade that she did carry safely to the picnic, and feel it quenching her thirst. She would take the trip again to the pavilion for the surprise, the chocolate ice cream—but it didn't end there. The best part was remembering the warmth of going with her mom and the young sisters she loved.

They didn't have much in material things; they were lucky they didn't know that or have a need for them. They had something else. Even though they became angry and often squabbled, they had each other and were a family trying to make it together!

Chapter 26

Clara Meets Max

Clara, like all mothers, thought her children were the most beautiful, and she always talked about getting a family picture, but somehow there was never the time or the money. Now, it became one of her priorities.

Until now, Clara had always sewn all the children's clothes, but for "the Picture" she was going to buy them dresses. Slovie's and Tobie's were alike; Rosie's, the little one's, was different.

Because money was scarce, Clara bought the dresses quite a bit larger, "for them to grow into." They were so large she had to take tucks in the skirts and tops to make them fit, but when she was finished, the girls thought they were the most beautiful dresses, probably in the whole world!

The week before picture taking, Clara, who was also the children's barber, cut their hair. She gave them Buster Brown haircuts (all the rage for children then), with bangs on the forehead and the sides longer, covering the ears. First she cut one side, then put a hand on their heads, holding the bowl in place while trying to cut the hair evenly around. Somehow, the bowl always moved, resulting in one side longer than the other. Their mother snipped the longer side, and by the time she got through the sides were almost the length of the bangs, way above the girls' ears. The children hated their haircuts and cried, "Mom, you're cutting too short!"

She'd reprimand them with, "Hold still! Just one more second. I'm almost finished." But they knew she could do a lot more damage, even in one second.

When she was through, they sulked as they stood back so she could review her handiwork. When she realized she had, indeed, cut it too short, she gave them this optimistic overview: "Don't worry. Hair grows fast!"

They hoped it would grow back before the picture was taken. Every day, they would look in the mirror to see if their hair had grown. They suffered with it. "Grow, please grow!" they coaxed as they pulled it down on the sides. Their hair wouldn't be hurried, and soon the "picture-taking Saturday" arrived.

At the photographer's, Clara was seated in a chair; then the man positioned the children, Rosie standing on the chair near Clara, and Slovie and Tobie on each side. The girls had their new dresses on, large taffeta bows on the tops of their heads, long white stockings, too large so they wrinkled, and button high-top black leather shoes. They stood there unsmiling—three serious-looking youngsters, apprehensive, anxiously staring at the photographer's mysterious draped box, not knowing what to expect.

The man put his head under the black cloth drape again and again. Then he called to them. "Look here, please smile," he coaxed, while he pressed the rubber bulb attached to a narrow, ropelike cord. The girls were too frightened to move; their eyes stared straight ahead. At last the ordeal was over and they went home, relieved. It hadn't been so bad after all.

Clara was very happy with the finished picture, an eight-by-ten. Clara looked beautiful, and the children, too. They had never seen a picture of themselves, so they were fascinated and studied it at great length. "Take it out. I want to see it!" It was passed back and forth until Clara put a stop to it.

"You'll get it dirty; then we won't be able to put it up," she warned.

She had an enlargement made and put it in an oval frame that matched the one with her wedding picture. She was so proud of it and stopped to look at it many times.

"Doos iz my farmeg [this is my fortune]." Her children were her fortune!

It was spring again, the spring of 1920. They were invited by one of Clara's friends for the Passover seder. Usually they were the only guests, but this time another guest was present, a man they had never seen before. He was short and stockily built, with a head of medium brown, curly hair, a mustache, and very dark brown eyes. He was most pleasant and spoke in a moderate tone of voice, but what Slovie remembered best about him was his face—jovial, covered with a big smile as if he were really enjoying himself. He was introduced as Max.

Max Sugarman was a widower. He had been married for ten years and never had any children. He was a shoe-repair man and owned his own shop, the Busy Bee Repair Shop. Most people found it hard to make ends meet, but small shop owners, working hard, were making it. Max was one of them.

The following week, Clara's friend came over to visit, and the two conversed in low tones. Whatever it was, Clara seemed pleased.

During that week Clara was alternately happy and humming and at other times seemed preoccupied. Early Sunday evening, Clara seemed nervous as she rushed the children through dinner and their baths. "Someone is coming over," she volunteered. "I have to go out for a little while, Slovie."

They heard the "someone" coming up the stairs and were surprised to see Max. Clara and Max exchanged greetings, a bit awkwardly. Max glanced around the room, hesitated a bit, then came over to the bed and gave the girls a bag of candy. "It's for all of you."

"You'll take care of your sisters, Sloveleh?" Clara phrased it as a question.

Clara's face was flushed as she and Max left. The children ran to the window to see them walking down the street and saw the neighbors craning their necks to watch also. Matchmakers were trying to pair Clara with Max, and this brought a little excitement to the neighborhood. There would be much contemplating and gossiping going on for the next few days.

The children got back into bed to divide the cache of candy. "Did you see him holding Mom's arm?" They giggled in approval.

Clara seemed to like Max. There was a little something different about her that week—the landlady's complaining didn't seem to bother her too much. She asked the children if they liked Max. Of course they did! Hadn't he brought the perfect icebreaker for children—candy?

At other times she worried out loud, "Ich vase nisht ahz ehr glacht mir [I don't know if he likes me]."

Clara really didn't know how pretty she was—beautiful on the outside, but her real beauty inside, in her warm heart, her understanding, her caring. She was always hopeful, ever the optimist. All her attributes made her a catch for a good man, a catch that would have to include the children.

The younger sisters were unaware of what was happening, but Slovie was six years old going on thirty. She was worried. She didn't know if she wanted Max to like her mother. What would that mean to all of them? What changes?

Max came a few times and took Clara out. The children liked him; he brought them candy and always took time to talk to them.

The courtship was short, and in the fall of 1920 Max married Clara, with her children! Max moved them to his home, which he owned. It was a lovely duplex, and they were to live in the five rooms downstairs. It was in a predominantly Jewish neighborhood with several grocery stores, butcher shops, and bakeries.

Max had come from Poland to escape the anti-Semitism there. Two of his landsmen lived next door. One, Pesach, had the Busy Bee Tailor Shop next to Max's shop. The two had a very close relationship. Pesach and his wife, Esther, married for many years, were childless. Esther and Clara became good friends.

While Clara was busy fixing up their new home, the children sat on the back porch playing dress-up with old dresses, hats, and jewelry, having the time of their lives. Clara came to the back screen door to watch them. She was all smiles as she stood there drying a fancy bowl and enjoying the pleasure of her children.

Max had hung the picture of Clara with her children in the living room. He loved that picture and showed it to all his friends. "Someday soon, we'll take a picture of all of us," he promised, and they were looking forward to that day.

Max couldn't do enough for his new family. When he came home after work, he was tired but always helped Clara, wanting to do whatever he could. "Don't lift that," he would say. "I'll do it for you."

At first the children were shy when Max was home, not knowing what to make of all the changes. They didn't know where exactly they could go and where they could not. They were so used to having boundaries set down, by the landlady. Max had never had any children, but he certainly understood them. He took them by the hand and led them into the living room. "This is your home," he told them. He was aware that they needed to feel they belonged, and he was tireless in his efforts to attain that goal. Wherever they sat, he came over to talk to them, interested in what they were doing. Soon they were very much at home with him.

Clara had been greatly concerned about this very matter, but she needn't have worried. She could see the difference in her children. They were happy and played well together, and she had time to spend with the "little one," so everybody thrived.

Their new home was a large place with a large living room and a beautiful dining room with a buffet that had two floor-length mirrors on the doors, one on either side of the cabinet part, which was filled with beautiful sparkly crystalware. The furniture in both rooms was very nice, and there were lovely rugs on polished floors.

There were two large bedrooms. The one off the dining room was for Clara and Max; the other one, off the kitchen, was for the girls. Slovie and Tobie slept in the larger bed on one side, and Rosie slept in the smaller one on the other side. For the first time they could remember, they were not crowded and could turn in bed without bumping the person next to them.

The kitchen was large, with a wonderful porcelain stove that had four burners and an oven to bake in, a kitchen set, and even a mirror on the wall over the big sink. It was nice to see so many mirrors in the house. In any room they walked by they could see themselves in a mirror—good, if one took this all in stride; bad, if one was predisposed to vanity.

They all loved the bathroom with its huge white porcelain tub that had claw feet and running water. The water went down a drain and didn't have to be thrown out.

Clara was so excited with her house, so full of all these wonders she had never had before. Every time she discovered a new one she would call out, "Come look, look at this!"

They hurried to look at the big pantry with its lovely dishes and glasses, and pots and pans hanging on the wall. There was a huge icebox in a separate room off the kitchen. It was so big. Clara wondered how much ice would go in there.

The front of the house had a large screened porch with black leather furniture in it. Small trees bordered the walk that led to the back of the house. The house and front yard were enclosed by a black wrought-iron fence with a swinging gate. There was a small garden filled with yellow and orange nasturtiums, and purple morning glories wrapped themselves around and climbed up the spokes of the fence.

Clara, who loved flowers, set aside a little time after dinner to water the flowers while Max sat on the porch reading the Jewish newspaper.

Clara was deliriously happy—in the morning and during the day the children could hear her singing a "Leidahleh" (a Jewish song) as she cleaned and scrubbed away. She couldn't be happier, and Max, too, was a happy man, so happy with his new family. They found him to be a most pleasant person—kind, soft-spoken, warm-hearted, and nice to be around.

When they got settled in, Clara took Tobie and Slovie to the new school—Slovie was entering second grade and Tobie first grade—the Hawthorne School, which went to the third grade.

Since an education had been denied Clara in Romania, school-ing was of the utmost importance to her. The day she took the girls to school was one of the happiest in her life. Her children could go to school in America. She always praised America—America, the Golden Land.

She had the greatest respect for school and teachers and instilled that in all of her children. At night, no matter how tired she was, she wanted to hear everything that happened in school. She would constantly admonish them with, "Be sure to listen to your teachers."

Slovie did as her mom said; she did her homework, struggling through, as there was no one at home who could help her. She bothered her teachers, constantly asking questions if she didn't understand, and there was much she didn't understand. Whatever she learned, she tried to teach her sisters. When chores were done after school, the children played school. Slovie was the teacher. An old orange crate was the teacher's desk. Slovie sat in front. The students, her two younger sisters, sat on the steps. Slovie gave them each a sheet of lined paper out of her precious tablet. The sheet was divided into two on each side. Half of one side of the sheet was used for arithmetic. The other half was used for spelling. On the opposite side half was for art, where they made pictures, and on the other half they learned to write words from the story the "teacher" read out of her schoolbook. The students liked the story reading best.

Clara enjoyed it, too. "Read to me," Clara would coax. Slovie read her schoolbooks to her mother as she did her ironing or cooking. It meant so much to Clara to hear her child read. "I'm so proud of you—if my mother, rest her soul, could only see you, she would be proud, too!"

Slovie always missed the grandmother she never knew, who her mother mentioned so often, and wished she could have known her. She sounded pretty special, and she made a great impact on the young girl's life. Her mother's encouragement made her try harder for both her mother and her grandmother.

They had been living with Max just a few months when the Red Cross got in touch with Clara. Several times Clara had made attempts to send mail to her family in Romania. She never heard anything but was hopeful, as the letters and parcels didn't come back.

After the war, the Red Cross was again helping her. It took a long time, so Clara was hopeful when she heard from them.

But the news was sad. No trace of the family—they and other villagers were presumed dead. Clara cried for days. Max tried to console her. He was there for her in so many ways. He sat with her, holding her hand. The children saw him sitting with Clara's head

142

on his shoulder, trying to comfort her, to ease her pain. Clara was sad for a long time. For sure now, she knew her family was gone.

Their first *Shabbos* with Max was a memorable one. Max insisted they eat in the dining room. "Why, Max? The dining room is for company."

Max got quite emotional. "You, all of you, are my company, my family! *Shabbos* we'll eat in the dining room!"

The house had been scrubbed for the Sabbath, and the children, too. Max and Clara sat like a king and queen, and there the children sat, like angels that night, the three little sisters. They were often sources of irritation for each other, with the squabbling and sibling rivalry, but Friday night they sat like angels.

Clara lit the candles and offered a Sabbath prayer. Her heart was filled with gladness for her Max and her family. When Clara took her hands from her face, tears were rolling down her cheeks. They were tears of joy. She looked at Max and in Max's eyes she saw his happiness. "Goot *Shabbos*," she said softly.

And they all answered, "Goot *Shabbos*!"

Max said the kiddush and then they started on the wonderful dinner Clara had prepared on the new stove. Max told her how good everything was. He smacked his lips in enjoyment. Everyone was happy.

Slovie sat where she could see the candles in the mirrors of the buffet. They golden-glowed like Midas's touch and brightened everything they cast their reflections on.

Max wanted the children to call him Papa Max. They said it over and over, "Papa Max! Papa Max!" His face lighted up with a wonderful satisfied smile as they said it. Slovie didn't have to be envious of other children anymore. Miracle of miracles, they were a real family.

The days spun into weeks, and the weeks into months, into the next year, when Clara became pregnant with Max's child. His happiness was such that words could not describe it. A religious man, he went to the synagogue and prayed. He thanked God for the blessings of his family, and now for the new life to come.

He went to work, hard work, with renewed vigor to earn a living for his family, and returned at night with such gladness in his heart. He was greatly concerned for his wife's well-being and hovered over her like the truly wonderful husband he was.

After dinner, when all had helped with the dishes, he insisted Clara rest and took all of the children for a walk and ice-cream cones.

They talked to Max about the baby. They were all so happy at the prospect of a new baby.

"What will the baby's name be?"

He wasn't sure yet about the first name, but the last name would be Sugarman, like his.

"Why can't our names be Sugarman, too?"

Max was surprised. "You want your name to be Sugarman?"

"Yes," they answered in unison.

"All right, we'll talk to Mom, and after the baby comes, we'll see to it that we're all Sugarmans!"

They practically bounced home to tell their mother!

On Sundays, after lunch, Max took the children to the Saint Francis Theater, so Clara could rest. The girls fought to take his hand and took turns. This pleased him, and he laughed good-naturedly, knowing they liked him, and he certainly reciprocated their feelings. They were wonderful little girls and gave him much joy and pleasure. He watched them at play and doing schoolwork, how they listened and learned from their older sister. They quarreled, but there was a deep love and affection for each other and their mother.

Their own father had not been a part of their lives. Clara had been their whole world. Now, they had everything—their mother and Max, their papa, a beautiful home—and they were a real family. Max made a big difference in their lives. Soon, he would have what he had always yearned for—a child of his own.

Max loved music. Sometimes, in the evening after dinner, Clara and Max sat in the living room. In one corner stood a beautiful mahogany phonograph. There was a case with shelves that held phonograph records of all kinds. The records came in paper covers to protect them from scratches. There were hundreds of them, and Max knew exactly which records were on which shelf. Max would choose different records: beautiful classical music, Jewish songs, operas, and Clara would listen as Max explained the operas, both in a world of their own, happy with each other.

The children came to respect his love for music, and it became part of their lives, too. They sat on the floor with papers and pencils, busy but quietly listening and enjoying this new world opened up to them.

Slovie later recalled, "I think we all had this feeling, but I can describe it only for myself. It was contentment. A certain calm had descended, removing the tension that had previously been a daily part of our lives. The tension had been there, but we were unaware of it; we just lived with it. Everything now was as it should be—Mom was home where she belonged, being a wife and mother.

"Not everyone knows what that feeling of contentment is like. To have it even once in a lifetime is indeed fortunate, a blessing! Mother had that feeling with Max—and so did we!"

Max and Clara waited impatiently for the new baby. As the pregnancy progressed, Clara blossomed and Max beamed.

At last their son was born, on June 6, 1922. Eight days after the birth the baby was circumcised (*bris*) and named Benjamin for Clara's father.

There was a little celebration with food—herring, crackers, cake, and wine. Everyone who came was happy for Max and Clara. They received congratulations and Baby Ben got gifts.

After everyone left, Max kept looking at the gifts for his son. He was so pleased, so happy. He sent Clara to bed to rest, then took the girls into the kitchen. Together they made dinner, happy Papa Max was letting them help, and they chattered like little magpies.

Thirty-one days after the birth of Baby Ben, another celebration was held (the *pidyon-ha-ben*, redemption of the firstborn male). Baby Ben was Max's firstborn son, so the special ceremony was held.

The neighbors brought the complete meal, and there was laughter and happiness and such merriment. Max had the phonograph playing happy Jewish songs and even joined in singing. All had a wonderful time, and when leaving, the guests wished the family years of happiness.

After everyone left, the family sat in the living room. Max sat in the big armchair, holding his son—looking at him, touching him, an air of wonderment about him. The girls sat on the davenport with their mother. Everyone was exhilarated. It had been a wonderful day!

Chapter 27

Tragedy

Life settled down with the new baby. The children played with him, took turns holding his little hands. His hair was light brown and showed a tendency to curl, and he captivated them all.

Papa Max came home every day for lunch and to spend time with Clara and his son. The girls sat on the porch or played hopscotch while they waited for him. When they saw him, they ran eagerly to meet him. He didn't forget them in the excitement of the new baby. He brought them long licorices or small boxes of multi-colored jells. Now Max received hugs from the girls and he hugged them back—big bear hugs.

After work, he couldn't wait to get home to hold Baby Ben. He talked to him. "Aren't you a wonderful baby, so small, but you'll grow big and strong."

Max, inexperienced with newborns, examined Ben thoroughly. One day he came home to find the baby had scratched his face with his tiny nail, one tiny scratch. Max was beside himself. Clara kept assuring him the baby would be fine. Max was a most doting father.

As before, Max took the girls out on Sunday so Clara could rest. This one Sunday they were particularly impatient to be off. Max was taking them to the shop; he had a few jobs to finish off, and they could watch him.

At the shop he answered their questions about everything, explaining how leather soles were sewn on shoes, as he demonstrated by running the huge machine. They saw him take an old pair of shoes, and when he finished with them they looked like new.

They learned how Max made his living for them. It was hard work, and before he was finished he was perspiring profusely from the work and the heat of the day.

Papa Max also sold new working shoes. Most of his customers were the policemen and firemen. They wore heavy black leather shoes. When they had to be repaired, the men brought them to the Busy Bee shop.

The shop was about two blocks from Saint Mary's Church, and both the sisters and fathers brought their shoes to be fixed.

Max was kept busy at the shop and was tired when he got home, but not too tired to give the girls a little of his attention, and then he spent time with the baby.

Once a week, on Thursdays after work, Papa Max and his two neighbors, Pesach and Morris, went out to farms, quite a way out in a rural area. They bought fresh chickens, eggs, and vegetables for their families.

One week in July they decided to go on a Wednesday night instead. They drove out in Morris's car. After they left, a summer storm erupted. The rain came down in a deluge. The lightning flashes lighted up the black night, thunder crashed, and strong winds shook the windows.

At home, the children became frightened, so Clara drew the shades. She sat down at the kitchen table to have a cup of tea. From her bed, Slovie could see her, glancing at the clock on the wall. The young girl came down to sit with her. She knew Clara was worried; it was very late, and Papa Max should have been home.

Most homes did not have phones; Max and the others couldn't get in touch with their families. Understandably, both the men and their families were quite concerned for each other's welfare during the violent storm.

Clara raised the shade and they all looked out into the blackness. A flash of lightning lit up the street, and they saw the rainwater, like a river, rushing down from the Mount Airy Hill, overflowing onto the sidewalks, washing down rocks of all sizes and wood and brush that became entangled in their iron fence.

Clara couldn't remember a storm as severe as this one. Another flash of lightning seemed to open up the sky, and they could see black clouds racing through. Clara pulled the shades and urged them to go back to bed.

Slovie didn't know how long they were asleep, but she was awakened by something. It was a knocking at the window in their room. Frightened, she listened and recognized Pesach's voice calling her mother. She pulled the shade. The rain had stopped, so she opened the window. When her eyes became accustomed to the dark, she could just barely make out Pesach, but she did see that his head was bandaged in white—a shocking, eerie sight in the night for anyone, especially a youngster.

She ran to wake her mother, and Clara hurried to open the door. Pesach's face was pale; he was shaking, and his voice trembled. "There's been an accident; Max is in the hospital."

Pesach told Clara how it had happened. The heavy rains had washed out some roads. They had thought about staying at a

147

farmhouse but decided to start back. Papa Max, who usually sat in front, wanted to sit in back to sleep. Another car had approached on the opposite side of the muddy road, veered across, and smashed into Max's side of the car with such force the car rolled over.

The others got out with only slight injuries, but Papa Max was pinned, crushed. The driver, drunk, escaped almost unscathed.

As Clara listened, she began to cry. "Oh, Max! Oh, Max!"

Grabbing anything she had handy, she dressed hurriedly while she gave Slovie instructions about the baby and younger girls. Then Pesach and Clara left to go by streetcar to Saint Joseph's Hospital.

In bed, Slovie mulled over Pesach's story. They had never heard of a car accident. They rarely saw cars except for the one next door, used mostly for Morris's business. Very few people had cars. Most traveled by streetcar, which was moderately expensive—five cents for the fare—or walked.

Slovie had never seen a person injured like Pesach, where his head had to be bandaged. She remembered thinking how terrible that was. She went to bed in her mother and Papa Max's bed to be near the baby, but it wasn't long before Tobie and Rosie crawled into bed, one on each side of her. They were upset and came to be comforted with hugs.

"What happened?" they wanted to know. Slovie tried to explain that Papa Max had been hurt and was in the hospital. The younger girls were talking, not understanding the seriousness of the situation. "He'll come home with Mom. We'll see him in the morning." They seemed very sure.

Slovie wasn't so sure. Pesach had been hurt on the head. Where was Papa Max hurt that he couldn't come home with Pesach? She didn't understand Pesach's description of Max's injuries— "crushed." What did that mean?

Morning came, and Clara hadn't returned. The children breakfasted and Tobie and Rosie went out to play, but they stayed on the front porch instead of going to their friends'. They were waiting for their mother and Papa Max.

When Baby Ben stirred and whimpered, Slovie took care of him as she had seen her mother do. He looked so little, so tiny. There was lunch and dishes, and the baby again, and it was getting late, on that afternoon in July.

Rosie saw her first. "Mom's coming!" she shouted.

Both the younger sisters tagged after their mother. She came in looking exhausted, terribly pale, and sweaty. It was a long, tiring walk from the streetcar, especially on a warm day.

They could see she had been crying. Nervously she kept rolling a very damp wadded-up handkerchief between her hands.

"Where's Papa Max?" they were anxious to know.

Clara's lips quivered. It was difficult for her to speak, and with much effort, she managed to impart the dreadful news.

"Papa Max is gone!"

They didn't fully comprehend it all, but seeing her and hearing her, they all began to cry with her.

They brought Papa Max home in a wooden coffin and set it on the living room floor. One man draped the casket with a black velvet cover that had a Star of David embroidered in gold thread on it and gold fringe that edged the cover that came down to the floor. Two candlesticks, with lighted tapers that flickered, casting shadows on the wall, were placed at the head of the coffin. There was no other light in the living room or dining room.

The news spread around the neighborhood like wildfire. Neighbors came to help, and there was a lot of commotion. One person was in charge of covering all the beautiful mirrors, shutting out a bright side of their lives.

They were all there in the kitchen and bedrooms, but the house took on an unusual quiet. Everything seemed hushed, strange, in this house that for a short time had known so much life.

Slovie and her younger sisters stood silently in the kitchen doorway looking at the coffin, knowing Papa Max was in it, but not wanting to believe it.

The *shammes*, a man from the synagogue, came in, took a chair, and sat between the living room and dining room. He would be there with Papa Max, so he would not be alone (according to the Jewish religion). The *shammes* would be there until the funeral.

Clara, who was inconsolable, spent much time in the bedroom or with the baby. The children seemed always to be in the way of the women who came to help to prepare the mourning meal for after the funeral. The children were constantly told to move, first here, then there.

With all this going on, frequently the fear in the younger sisters would manifest itself into tears. Rosie wanted to sit on Slovie's lap, and Tobie just wanted to be near Slovie. They went into the bedroom and shut the door. It afforded them a little privacy, where Slovie consoled them, even though she was frightened, too. No one paid any attention to them; no one missed them.

That night when people had gone, they all went to bed exhausted. Slovie heard her mother sobbing and asking questions: "Max, Max, why did you leave us?"

It made Slovie so unhappy to hear the pain and despair in Clara's voice. she got out of bed, quietly, so as not to awaken her little sisters, and went to her mother. She saw her kneeling at the coffin, so forlorn, so alone, overcome with grief.

Slovie took her mother's hand. It was cold and clenched shut. Slowly Slovie forced it open and put her hand in it.

"Mom. Can I sleep with you?"

There was no answer. Slovie didn't know if Clara even heard, so she went back to bed.

Later, she heard her mother still crying. Slovie came to Clara's bed and got under the covers, put her arms around her, and hugged her. She felt the tears wet on her cheek. Slovie wiped them away. She loved her mother but couldn't help her. She didn't know what to say or what to do. She felt helpless.

"Oy Mamaleh," her mother cried. "Zis inz getroffen ah zah imglik! [Such a tragedy has befallen us!]"

Slovie felt a lump rising in her throat. She held her mother for a long time, even after the arm under her mother's head had gone numb.

Sunday morning came, the day of the funeral. Clara cried as she took care of Baby Ben. Mahshie, a neighbor, came in, took one look, and took the baby from her. Another neighbor came in with food. "The hearse is here," she announced in a low voice to Mahshie. The pallbearers came in and Clara burst into tears again when she saw them go to Max.

The casket seemed very heavy, and the pallbearers struggled as they lifted it from the floor. When they started toward the door, Clara grew faint, and a neighbor standing near steadied her and slowly they followed the casket out.

The children, downcast, stood there watching the solemn scene unfolding. Curious onlookers, people from the neighborhood, crowded the sidewalk. A few were grave and somber, some were just gawking, but some were talking and laughing. This was difficult for Slovie to understand. She wondered what kind of people derived pleasure seeing someone else's misfortune. What made people so uncaring?

While the casket was being lifted into the hearse, Clara sat on the steps. She felt very weak, mentally and physically fatigued. She was so young, dressed in black, her face so pale and sad, she looked as if she were in the wrong place and didn't belong here at this sorry spectacle.

Slovie kept thinking, *All this is happening because of a car. A car did this to Max and us!* She grew up hating cars!

Slovie wanted to go with her mother to the cemetery, but her mother said she couldn't go.

"Sloveleh, I need you to watch Tobie and Rosie, and the baby, too, 'til I get back." Her voice broke and tears welled and fell. That Sunday was a warm, dismally gloomy day; it looked like rain at any moment. Slovie saw her mother shiver.

With Max, Clara's life had begun to feel whole again. Now, it was agonizingly torn apart. The future she and Max had talked about, looked forward to with such hope, was gone, with one swift, horrible blow. Why did this have to happen to Max? He had so endeared himself to all of them. He was such a good person; bad things are not supposed to happen to good people. They couldn't understand it. Their life had been so good; they thought it would go on forever.

Later Slovie, when remembering it all, thought, *Wouldn't it have been wonderful if time* had *stopped for us at that happy period in our lives—if that could have gone on forever?*

Unfortunately, life isn't like that. It doesn't stand still. There are always changes; nothing is permanent.

The next month was an excruciatingly painful one for Clara. She was consumed with so many feelings, so many questions. Why? Why did Max go that night, Wednesday, instead of Thursday? When the storm hit, why didn't they stay overnight? Max never sat in the back of the car. Why did he that night? Question after question tortured her. Do men make their own decisions, or are they already made for them? There was much to ponder, and no answers.

No one knows how many go through a lifetime with no real happiness. God had been good; He had given Clara and her children almost two years of it with Max, their Papa Max.

Slovie later analyzed it thus: "Our early emotional haven was the result of that incredibly wonderful family connection. Our world had been a caring world, and for a short time we tasted what life could be."

No matter what happened in their lives after that, they could always look back on that time when they were a loving family, the family Clara had always wanted, with a loving husband and her children.

They always hoped somehow Papa Max knew how life with him,

though very brief, had impacted their lives. Young as they were, it would sustain each of them. They would talk about it, and remember it often, through their lifetimes.

Max had never adopted them, giving them his name. There hadn't been time even to take the promised family portrait. The family had no picture of Max, but images of him were indelibly printed on their minds and in their hearts!

Chapter 28

A Family Coping

After a week, the mirrors were uncovered and it was time for Clara to pick up the fragments of her life. There was the shoe repair business to learn, the house to take care of, the tenant upstairs, taxes, and bills—all quite intimidating for the young widow.

The shop would be the livelihood for Clara and the children; therefore, her concern for the immediacy of getting started was understandable. The shop had to be reopened.

It was a foregone conclusion that Slovie would stay home with her sisters while her mother went to meet the new challenges. These events that had happened in Clara's life shortened Slovie's childhood, and she grew up quickly. More responsibilities seemed to be a natural progression for the child—caretaker and protector of her siblings. Now there would be the shop.

The shop had been closed for a week, the *shiva* week. Customers stopped in to offer their condolences, others to tell Clara what a fine person Max had been.

It made her sad that he was gone, but she was proud that she had married him and that now so many were affirming what she had known from the first.

Customers came to have their shoes repaired, but Clara didn't have a shoe repairman. Max had done that himself. So the customers went elsewhere, and Clara was losing much-needed business. She feared she wouldn't make her expenses for the month.

It took another week before Clara found a shoe repairman to hire. His name was Mr. Johnson. He spoke with a Norwegian accent that sometimes was a little difficult to understand. He was slightly built, graying, and middle-aged, a funny little man who wore gold wire-rimmed glasses set down near the end of his nose. When he spoke to you, he peered over the top of his glasses, which raised his eyebrows and gave his face a quizzical expression.

Good shoe repairmen usually kept their jobs until they died or became ill, so Clara questioned Mr. Johnson closely as to why he was unemployed. He told her he had been ill for a long time; she had no reason to doubt his story.

Clara gave Mr. Johnson a trial run for a week to see how he

would do. She bought the best materials—the best leather for soles and the best rubber heels—and Mr. J., as Mr. Johnson preferred to be called, did a really fine job. Quality work and quality materials went out from the Busy Bee, as Papa Max would have wanted it.

Clara was so pleased when customers told her how satisfied they were—a satisfied customer, she learned, was the name of the game. That meant repeat business from loyal customers.

Max had done his own work, so the shop had made him a good living, but Clara had to pay Mr. J. a fair salary because of his excellent work, and this meant a substantial reduction in her income. To the small display case that carried shoelaces and shoe polish, Clara now added men's leather belts and coin purses, hoping to increase sales.

There were new hardships for Clara; she got up early every morning, taking six-week-old Baby Ben to the shop, rushing to get there by six o'clock. She fairly flew with the baby carriage, because the Landis machine had to be started early. The ugly six-foot-tall machine was used to sew leather soles. A rock-hard block of wax, the size of a red building brick, had to be melted in it; the hot wax was essential to sewing the thick, heavy thread through the leather. Clara and Mr. J. took turns pushing and prodding the brick of wax, hoping it would melt faster, but it took its time.

Sometimes when the machine wore on Mr. J.'s patience, he would rave and rant and swear. Then he would pester Clara to let him go to the saloon two doors away; he needed "a little drink."

Mr. J. liked to drink, not "a little"; he drank a lot and then would not show up for work for a day or two. Clara learned why Mr. J. didn't have a job when she first met him. His "illness" was drinking.

She learned never to let him out of her sight once he got to work. He had lunch at the shop, eating Clara's cooking, and he stayed until closing time. He got paid on Saturday; then everyone prayed he would show up on Monday. Most of the time he did, but once in a while, when least expected, Mr. J. took his little "vacation."

When he came back, he looked sheepish and embarrassed and felt guilty because the shop had lost business. The shoe repair jobs were piled high on the counter, and he worked like a Trojan trying to complete as many as he could. He would apologize over and over, knowing Clara was angry with him.

This was the first time Clara had to deal with another person working for her. It was very difficult for her when she had to reprimand Mr. J. for anything. First of all, he was older than she was, and as she said, "I feel like I'm doing it to my father." Many times she didn't scold him when he really deserved it, but she realized that she was running a business. She had to keep her kindhearted feelings out of it. "Business is business!" she said. There were so many things to learn. She did, and ran the Busy Bee well!

Clara kept her ears open for information that might lead to another repairman. In the meantime, Mr. J. worked, sometimes for months, before it was time for his whiskey bender; then off he would go.

Clara couldn't trust him to go for supplies. He would stop at the first saloon he came to, and she couldn't leave him alone in the store, so the job of getting supplies fell to Slovie.

The first time Slovie went, she found the place to be quite a distance from the shop. The streets were unfamiliar to her, and she worried she would get lost. She tried to concentrate on Mr. J.'s directions, and came to Saint Mary's Church, as he had said. The church doors were open, so she looked inside the mysterious cavern of a Catholic church.

The church was dark, but she could see the pews and, at the end of the long aisle, the huge, brightly colored glass windows, beautiful with the light shining through. So engrossed in the images in the window was she, she didn't notice the sister standing near her. Slovie was so embarrassed when she saw her, as if she had been caught intruding in a place she didn't belong. The sister smiled at her, but off she ran.

So many sisters came to have their shoes repaired, and Slovie heard her mother and Mr. J. discuss them. Her mother wanted to know all about them—about the heavy habits they wore even in summer, what they wore underneath them, and what they did all day in church. Mr. J. would answer the questions, and their discussions were long. Slovie found them interesting and informative but did not fully comprehend the different religion.

"Sisters," Clara explained, "are very good people, always helping others." When they came to the store, they were always so polite, and she addressed them with great respect as "Sister."

"What can I help you with today, Sister?" she would say.

When they left, they always said a blessing to the children, if they were around, and to Clara. Clara would answer with, "Thank you, Sister." The children learned to respect people of other religions.

Slovie had taken too much time at the church, so she ran the rest of the way and finally saw the huge gold letters of the "Nicholas, Dean and Gregg" sign that marked her destination. She hesitantly walked up the broad, long steps that led to the interior. There were no women, only men seated at desks, busily writing in ledgers or reading the numerous files stacked on their desks. They were working very hard, heads bent in concentration. Slovie received her order and remembered to get the receipt marked "Paid" as her mother had instructed her.

The distance walking to the door seemed shorter than when she had come in. For some reason, the building and those in it didn't seem so formidable now.

Sometimes Slovie took her younger sisters with her so they could learn to get the supplies, too. The youngsters all gained confidence. Challenges, they found, were not so frightening once they set about meeting them. The children saw how people worked at so many different jobs. Early in life, they learned the "hard work code ethic."

It was important that the younger ones learn some of the jobs. That released Slovie to do other things.

There was the time Baby Ben caught a cold and it developed into pneumonia. He ran a high fever and was ill and listless. The doctor fixed a tent over Ben's little crib, and Clara brought endless numbers of teakettles of boiling water to fill the makeshift tent with steam to ease his labored breathing. She was with him constantly, day and night, while the fever raged mercilessly and took its toll of the tiny body. His sisters hovered near his room, hoping he would get well. The doctor came and stayed for hours, speaking little, looking grim. The house wasn't the same with Baby Ben ill.

The crisis came in the night. The fever broke and Clara wept. She had prayed with all her heart and soul for her son, "Please, God, let him live." God had been good and answered her prayers, and Clara, in thankfulness, went to the synagogue.

During this family emergency, Slovie got the chance to learn about the shop. She got up early and waited for Mr. J. to show up to start the furnace and the hot wax in the machine.

At the store Slovie learned the many jobs that had to be done besides repairing the shoes. The store and front walk had to be swept and chairs and counters dusted. She learned how to prepare tickets for shoes to be repaired—one-half tied to the shoes, the shoes tied together, and the bottom stub given to the customer so he could redeem his shoes.

Slovie had watched her mother and Mr. J. do this hundreds of times, almost automatically. Now she learned it took concentration so the shoes wouldn't get mixed up. So many of them looked the same, the black leather shoes of the policemen and the firemen.

Slovie enjoyed helping these customers. They were nice people. Sometimes they teased her about not being in school, the policemen telling her she could go to jail. The first one to say that to her had her almost in tears. She and her sisters had been taught to have respect for these wonderful public servants, and Slovie thought he was telling her the truth. Then Mr. J. winked at her and said the policeman was only fooling. What a great relief that was for a nine-year-old!

Clara dictated the excuses for absence from school. Slovie wrote them, and Clara signed them. She had learned to write her name for signing checks and business papers. The teachers knew of the family's problems but didn't excuse Slovie from homework, whether she was absent or not. It had to be in on time. There were extenuating circumstances for missing school; that couldn't be altered, and the family was coping to the best of their abilities.

At the store, Slovie learned to take payments and count out change, under Mr. J.'s watchful eye. She carried the key to the cash register on a string around her neck so she wouldn't lose it, and so Mr. J. couldn't get into it for drinking money.

When Slovie first came to the store she followed her mother's system for keeping the account of the day's receipts. Slovie stood on a box behind the counter so she could reach the top. On a two-inch-by-twenty-four inch strip of brown wrapping paper she laboriously wrote the cash amounts received in one column. People didn't write checks then. The sales ran from $.05 for two pairs of shoelaces to $5.95 for new shoes. She wished there were more shoes sales, because they added so much more money to the column and made her mother feel better.

At the end of the day, Slovie deducted the expenses for the day, which once in a while included $.15 for the lunch her mother said she could have at Mr. Constantin's Greek restaurant in the middle of the block. The lunch was a real treat—three blueberry pancakes and a tall glass of chocolate milk, free, courtesy of Mr. Constantin.

At the end of the day Slovie closed the shop and walked home. It was still light out in summer, but dark, cold, and sometimes snowing in winter. She liked to walk home in the dark and look into store windows with their bright lights, especially at Christmastime, when there were toys and beautiful porcelain-faced dolls.

One time she picked out what she thought was the prettiest doll in the window and wished Santa Claus would make a mistake and drop it down their chimney even though she was Jewish. But he never did, and she wondered how he knew which houses were Jewish and which were not.

On the way home she had to stop at the bakery shop. Halfway down the block, she could see the glow of the beckoning bakery lights casting shadows on the newly fallen snow. A bell tinkled when she opened the door, summoning someone from the back room. The warmth of the ovens felt good, and the smell of the freshly baked bread greeted her nostrils as she took a long, most satisfying, deep breath. She looked at the tempting sugared jelly doughnuts in the case, wanting one, but bought only the *challah* her mother had asked her to bring home.

As she made her way home along Canada Street, her face brightened when she saw the glowing orange Hanukkah candles in the many Jewish homes. She had forgotten it was the first night of Hanukkah and began to walk a little faster. She knew they were waiting for her at home to open the gifts their mother had for them.

When she got to the gate, she could see her mother and sisters in the window watching for her. Eagerly they met her at the door. "Hurry! Hurry!"

First they lighted the candles and then sat down to eat potato *latkes* (pancakes), the traditional Hanukkah food.

Clara kept refilling the platter with the crisp golden-brown delicacy until the others complained that they were all stuffed. Then obligingly they all helped clear the table as the brown-paper packages tied in colored embroidery thread were set in the middle of the table.

Clara handed them out to the children. They "ohed" and "ahed" at the warm scarves and mittens Clara had made—red for Rosie, purple for Tobie, pink for Slovie, and yellow for Baby Ben. They put them on and went to look in the mirror.

"Thanks, Mom!" They scrambled to kiss her, so happy with their gifts.

Slovie relayed all the day's happenings to her mother, answering all the questions about the shop.

Clara looked in wonderment at this child—more a grown-up than a child—a friend and confidante, too!

School homework had to be done, and finally tired from the excitement of *Hanukkah*, they were in bed wearing their new scarves and mittens.

After school the girls went to the store to take Baby Ben out to give him some fresh air. He spent most of his days in the store with the smells of leather and polishes and the rubber cement used for soles. He was pale and a frail youngster after his bout with pneumonia but was the most good-natured little boy—a joy to take care of.

There were always a few chores to do at home—dishes, dusting, whatever Clara needed done. The girls took turns or worked together and most of the time everything went smoothly, but every once in a while, as in other households, the siblings didn't get along. There were arguments, fighting, squabbling, and bickering. Tobie constantly picked on her younger sister, Rosie. Slovie had to step in and referee, angrily chastising Tobie for striking and really hurting her younger sister. The "little one" fought back and held her own.

Each generation tries to make things better for their children than the last. Clara, tough as things were, tried to give her children opportunities she never had. There wasn't much extra money to spend, but Clara wanted her children to learn Hebrew.

She hired a rabbi, Rabbi Katz, to come in once a week in the evening. He was quite elderly, and by the time he finished with his other pupils and got to their house, he was a very tired rabbi.

The girls each had a fifteen-minute lesson and then were to practice and write the lesson for the following week in their study books. He sat with each of them as they read, turning the pages for the rabbi, who dozed off frequently. They read on, their mother listening in the next room: "Ah, aw, eh, ee, bah, baw, beh, bee," a brave attempt to learn the Hebrew alphabet.

When they thought the rabbi was sound asleep they would turn two pages at a time to skip some of the monotonous lesson. Immediately, as if a warning bell had gone off in his head, the poor rabbi was wide awake, angrily turning back the pages, saying "*Zog! Zog!* [Read! Read!]" They couldn't fool that rabbi and didn't try it very often.

They had different lessons because of their ages. The younger ones didn't do their lessons or study, and Rabbi would scold them. After a year Clara stopped the lessons.

There is love of nature inside all of us. Clara had taught her children to love flowers; now she was planting a vegetable garden. The children watched her plant carrots, radishes, corn, garlic, and onions. Peas and beans climbed up on the strings she had nailed to the back fence.

The children helped with the digging of small holes, even the "little one," Rosie, helped. They dropped the seeds in the holes, carefully covering them and then watering them.

Every day they went out to see if anything had come up, and day after day were disappointed. At last one day there were rewards, tiny green stems sprouting, struggling to make it through the earth. Their mother came to see and called this "another of God's miracles."

Patiently all waited for the day when they could pick the fruits of their labor. They were always so excited to grasp a green fernlike top and pull up an orange carrot, or pull up the wide leaves and come up with a red radish. Carefully they washed them and bit into them—sweet, crisp, and crunchy! They wondered how it all happened. They had put in different-colored, different-shaped seeds and didn't understand how they were turned into the vegetables. For them it was a mystery, to their mother "one of God's wonders!"

Two years had passed since Papa Max had died. For some weeks no one had talked about him in front of Clara, because she would cry. Then she began to speak of him; it was good for all to talk of him, because there were so many wonderful things to say and remember.

Many had doubted Clara could take care of the business, but she surprised all the doubting Thomases, doing fairly well in the store, dealing with the customers and Mr. J.

The children were doing well in school, which made Clara so proud, and they were growing up.

Clara believed in busy hands and busy minds, so she didn't let too much time elapse after the rabbi incident before she bought a piano, making the minimal monthly payments. The children didn't know how, but she managed to find them a music teacher, a spinster lady, very prim and proper. They called her Miss Woods. Miss Woods was of a serious mind, and the sisters had to quit their giggling. She kept her hat on all the while she was teaching. Her hat had huge hat pins, a long one in front and a long one in back. Sometimes when she leaned forward to show the girls how a certain exercise was played, her hat pin would catch on their hair ribbons. She would struggle to get it released but then had to take her hat off. Then she would become so tense, you could feel her body stiffen up, and she would look more serious than before.

Clara paid her fifty cents for Tobie's and Slovie's lessons. Miss Woods, near the end of the lesson, would tinkle off the new exercise for the following week. It always sounded wonderful, melodious and effortless, when she played it.

During the week they were supposed to practice fifteen minutes a day. Poor Miss Woods came the next week and listened to their miserable attempts at a lesson that wasn't practiced.

She had difficulty even recognizing the music they valiantly struggled through.

This fiasco went on for nearly a year before Clara, busy with the shop, became aware that her children were no Paderewskis, so Miss Woods lost two pupils. She couldn't have minded too much! The girls must have exasperated the poor woman no end, and it was probably the hardest she ever worked to earn fifty cents!

When Slovie grew older, she appreciated the piano more. She bought piano books and practiced and practiced. Miss Woods had given them a good base. Slovie finally learned to play "The Skater's Waltz," "The Blue Danube," "Polonaise," and other songs that were, wonder of wonders, recognizable! Playing the piano afforded Slovie many relaxing hours of beautiful music. She often wished she could have said to Miss Woods, "Thank you, Miss Woods. It wasn't all in vain."

The family learned to cope by observing their mother—how she met life's day-to-day problems. Nothing was put off. She faced the challenges head-on and tried to work them out. She had to make decisions, and made them. Some were good; some weren't—if she couldn't change things, she lived with the outcome and didn't complain or blame anyone. From her they learned to accept what they couldn't change!

Chapter 29
New Chain of Events

Summer had gone, with its sweltering days and mosquito-filled nights; the fall school year had begun and the Rosh Hashanah and Yom Kippur holidays were upon the community.

This was a sad time of year for Clara as she went to the synagogue for the *yiskor* ("remember") service for Max and her parents. In the synagogue, the women and girls sat upstairs separated from the men and boys downstairs. Grieving, again, at the memorial service, Clara was always strengthened whenever any of her children came to sit with her. Today she saw her Slovie coming toward her.

The young girl had been up here on another holiday and had looked down, trying to find Papa Max. Her face would brighten when she caught a glimpse of him wearing his tallith on his shoulders and yarmulke on his head. He was a source of pride to her, and such an important part of her life. She had loved him, her Papa Max!

She had watched him as he *davened*, and when he glanced up to where she and her mother were sitting, there had been a sense of quiet contentment.

Now Slovie looked down and saw others in his place, and she felt only a large emptiness because Papa Max was missing. His passing left an aching void that would never be filled.

Everyone was standing, caught up in chanting the prayers, when a loud commotion at the doors interrupted the service. The women began whispering, "It's those devils again!"

The opened doors were quickly shut and remained so until the congregants began to leave. They were met with a barrage of stones and rocks and, accompanying them, loud taunts of: "Christ killers! Christ killers!"

Clara tried to cover Slovie's head to protect her as they hurried out. Slovie recognized some of the culprits as members of the Mount Airy Gang! Tough boys and girls, they always had fights with kids in the neighborhood, youngsters who were no match for them. They were bullies, threatening and taking advantage of younger children.

This, however, was different. This was hate, vicious hate! It could be seen in their faces as they threw their well-aimed rocks, striking the worshipers. Many came away with bruises and injuries. This incident of hate Slovie was witnessing was something new and made a deep impression on her. It stayed in her mind.

"What do they mean, Mom? Who was Christ? Who killed him?"

Clara had come to America to be free of anti-Semitism, but now here in this neighborhood where life once had been good, the ugly scepter of hate was raised again. Clara tried to explain the hate some people have for Jews. She never thought she would have to impart this to her children, and it hurt her deeply.

"But not all people are like that," she hastened to add, trying to dispel some of her child's fear.

This was Slovie's first brush with anti-Semitism. She had nightmares about soldiers, soldiers with faces of the Mount Airy Gang, riding horses, attacking her with swords. She fought them through the night, running between the galloping steeds, cut and bloody. The more she fought, the more enemy soldiers appeared, and she would wake up in a cold sweat, crying until her mother came to comfort her.

Slovie was remembering the anti-Semitic attacks in Romania her mother had always told her about. She asked, "Do you think it will happen here like in Romania, Mom?"

"No, no!" her mother assured her. "They won't come here; that was a long time ago." Clara voiced that to her child, but in her heart she wasn't absolutely sure anymore. Sometimes there were talks about "incidents." The hate was here, too, in America!

As Slovie grew up she learned how the hate, through ignorance and bigotry, would manifest itself many times in outbreaks like this one, and worse ones, and in other ways more subtle.

People lived with it, pretending it didn't exist, and complainers were labeled as "Jews too sensitive about being Jews!"

After the holidays, people began thinking of winter. The *Farmer's Almanac* had predicted a colder-than-usual winter with lots of snow, cold winds, and freezing temperatures. Most everyone paid attention to what the *Farmer's Almanac* had to say. In the Midwest, to farmers, businessmen, and others, it was as important as or even more important than the Bible!

People in the neighborhood were preparing for winter—Clara and neighbors cleaned the storm windows and hung them up, coal trucks delivered the briquettes, and cut wood was hauled in and stacked. Busy squirrels, gathering and scurrying for weeks, and fat woolly caterpillars were other telltale signs that winter would be a rough one.

Clara spent her evenings knitting warm caps, scarves, and mittens while she and the neighbors speculated on what, and how much, to set aside in their winter cellars.

This all was of great concern to Mr. O'Brien. He was one of the firemen from the nearby station. He, and most of the other firemen, happened to be Irish and good family men, so there was much to talk about. Clara inquired about their families and knew which ones were expecting babies and which ones were ill, and many of the firemen told her about other serious problems. They found her to be a good listener.

Mr. O'Brien opened the door on a cold, blustery fall day, and the strong northwesterly wind almost blew him into the shop. His coat collar was pulled way up around his neck to ward off the cold wind and the light flurry of snowflakes, early harbingers of what was to come.

He opened his coat and came over to the heat register, while he blew into his cold hands to warm them.

" ' Twas the cold weather forecast in the almanac," he said, "that brought me in to get a new pair of shoes."

When the store wasn't busy, Clara took a moment or two to chat with the customers as she did on this particular day with Mr. O'Brien. Sometimes they needed shoes or shoes repaired, and when they were short of money because of a family crisis, Clara gave them credit until their next paycheck. They considered her a friend, and for that reason Mr. O'Brien had come with good news for her. The firemen in his station had convinced other firemen to get their new shoes, or old shoes repaired, at the Busy Bee. Clara, of course, was so appreciative and thanked him over and over, ending with, "God bless you and your family, Mr. O'Brien."

Mr. O'Brien was a strict Catholic, but he didn't seem to mind Clara's Jewish God blessing him, too. When Mr. O'Brien left that day, he had no way of knowing what chain of events his good deed would set in motion.

Before too long the new customers from the other engine houses did come. This meant Clara had to increase the stock of new shoes. Max had purchased new shoes from a Mr. Mintz, and Clara had continued that business connection, since it had been profitable for the Busy Bee.

The sale of one or two extra pairs of shoes every week meant the new shoe business was fast becoming an important part of the store.

Where before the shop had four chairs for customers, set off in a small space to one side, the newly expanded shoe department now proudly boasted six chairs and a piece of rug. Even Mr. J., with great zeal and ardor, went to work sawing and nailing more shelves on which to stack the boxes of new shoes.

Mr. Mintz, the shoe salesman, now came once and sometimes twice a week. It was because of his more frequent calls that the children took note of him. He seemed to be at the store all the time. He was a short man, mostly because of a back deformity that made him appear a little hunchbacked. His head was bald on top, and his hair, what there was of it, a little on each side, was gray. He dressed neatly, was very businesslike and serious-minded, didn't say too much, and seldom smiled. He was an older man, probably in his early fifties.

Slovie came to the store one day to find her mother patiently waiting for her. Mr. O'Brien's good deed was working overtime. Clara had an order for six pairs of new shows. Clara had promised them for the next day and always tried to keep her word. This meant she had to make a special trip to Mr. Mintz's store. Since Clara couldn't read, Slovie had to go with her to read the signs on the streets and streetcars.

They came by streetcar over the Robert Street Bridge, which crossed the Mississippi River, and got off on Fairfield Avenue. Mr. Mintz's shop was on the left side of the street, a very small shop in an area known as the West Side. They visited for just a short time, just to get their order, and left.

The increased business pleased Clara. Her life was one round of work after another and she wasn't ever free of worry and responsibility for her children, but she was thankful and felt blessed because, as she said, "My children are good and a big help to me."

The winter came howling in, and yes, that darned almanac was right again. The cold Canadian winds fought their way around the houses, which creaked and groaned from the onslaught, and the freezing temperatures spiraled ever downward.

It snowed so much, day after day after day, that the weight of the snow caused the collapse of the Franklin School's roof. It caved in, the wood and stone and ice and snow falling downward, resulting in considerable damage to several floors. The good part was that the children had weeks of an unplanned vacation; the bad part was that the poor parents had a miserable time stuck inside with irritable children who couldn't go out because of the abominably cold weather. When it ended, parents were of one accord: "Teachers aren't paid enough to take care of the little rascals."

Eventually that all passed and the spring everyone was looking forward to was on its way. The sun came out and stayed longer, the snow disappeared, storm windows came down and screens went up again. People were preparing for Passover and Easter. The shop needed more shoes, and Mr. Mintz came more often.

One Friday night Mr. Mintz came for dinner. Clara had also invited Pesach and Esther. During the week Clara had mentioned to Esther that Mr. Mintz was a widower and lived alone.

The children all sat on one side, opposite the adults. Company had not been in the house since Papa Max died. With all the company at the table, Papa Max was missed. They looked at each other and knew their thoughts were the same. Quietly they groped for hands to hold. When they needed comfort and support, there were always each other's hands to hold.

The matchmakers had not been idle. They had introduced Clara to a very nice man, and he had called on her just a few times. They went to the cinema and sometimes to see live Jewish theater, which Clara loved.

Now Mr. Mintz became a visitor, too, and young as they were, the children knew things were not the same anymore. With two suitors, changes were brewing. The rivals tried to outdo each other with bigger, better boxes of chocolates. It wasn't difficult to discern the rivalry between them.

Mr. Mintz liked Clara very much and, a jump ahead of the other interested party, asked Clara to marry him. She didn't accept right off, and he was terribly disappointed. The discussion went on for hours. She had to give this proposal of marriage some thought. She was young but didn't know if she wanted to be married again. Things were difficult for her in many ways, but facets of her life had fallen into place and she was content with her home and work and children.

There was much for her to consider. Mr. Mintz was twenty-two years her senior. Clara was just thirty and a very pretty young woman.

There was much to discuss—the children, the Busy Bee, and their home These were all major concerns of hers. Mr. Mintz had two grown children: a son from whom he had been estranged for many, many years and a married daughter. He had discussed the marriage with the daughter, and she had opposed it with many arguments. His age, for one thing—he was fifty-two. She considered him an old man, too old to get married again and take a family of four children. Her arguments may have been valid, but he didn't put much store in them.

The following week, the children overheard the conversations Mr. Mintz had with their mother. He had come one night, quite upset with his family.

"My daughter does not understand how difficult it is for me alone."

He had countered with his arguments—he would be getting a nice wife, and there was a home they would live in, much better than his crowded quarters. He would sell his small shop and take charge of the Busy Bee, which was more profitable. The children his family was so concerned about were good children.

However, to avoid involvement in his family situation, Clara decided it was probably best for her and Mr. Mintz not to see each other anymore. Needless to say, he was very unhappy with the decision. He cared for Clara.

Clara was angry about anyone saying anything against her children. They were growing up, and having lived with Max, she knew she wanted the stability of a good husband and father and (this was considered normal) she yearned to be home with the children. What she desired was what she had always longed for—to be part of a family again!

After quite a few months, Mr. Mintz came again, and after much deliberation on Clara's part, together with Mr. Mintz's incessant pressuring, Clara chose to accept his proposal, although she did it with much trepidation. They were married at the rabbi's house, over the objections of Mr. Mintz's daughter. Pesach and Esther were the obliging witnesses.

To outward appearances, all seemed well now that Clara and Mr. Mintz were married, but his family never accepted Clara and her children, which caused many problems. Clara and the children called him Pa, and he came to live with them. It was a big change for the children, having someone new coming into their home, and it must have been difficult for him, getting used to four youngsters.

Things went along smoothly some days; others were a bit more hectic. Every morning Pa Mintz left for his store and Clara went to hers. As the months went by and cold weather was looming ahead, traveling back and forth for him became a bit difficult. Clara had hoped his shop would have been sold by now, but there were no prospects.

It was almost two years into the marriage when Clara found she was pregnant with her fifth child. Pa Mintz now wanted Clara to sell the Busy Bee and move to the West Side. It was an absurd demand and angered her, since it was contrary to their premarriage discussions and plans. Those had not been haphazard discussions and had been considered serious by both of them.

He didn't tell Clara why he had changed his mind. He didn't have to. She knew it was family interference. The ensuing arguments were frequent—voices raised in resentment and anger, which sickened Clara. Nothing was resolved.

After weeks of this unpleasant atmosphere in their home, Clara made the decision to sell the store. It broke her heart to do it; it had meant so much to her. Somehow, she hoped by acceding to his wishes, things would be better. No matter how dismal things appeared, Clara was the eternal optimist, always reconciled to doing the best and going on.

Everyone who knew the Busy Bee said it would fetch a good price, and it did. Clara gave the money to Pa to open a bigger place to develop more business. He rented the vacant shop across from his store. They increased their stock, and the balance was put in the bank to save toward a house.

Clara missed the store, especially when Pesach told her so many customers wanted to know why she sold it. She didn't afford herself the luxury of postmortems. What was done was done. There was no time or energy to waste on yesterdays. Concentration had be salvaged for the todays and tomorrows.

Clara hated the thought of strangers living in the place where she and Max and the children had been so happy, but now she was married to Pa Mintz and he wanted the family moved to the West Side. She ran an ad and when the first prospective tenants arrived, it was difficult for her to show them her home. Of course, the beautiful place rented immediately.

Clara had weighed the reasons to go, but the reasons to stay were decidedly overwhelming. Principal was Pa's going back on his word. She couldn't forget he had broken his promise to her, even knowing how important it was to her and the children.

Esther and Pesach didn't want her to move, either. They had been good friends, and Clara and her family had become important to them. Clara had been hurt, her faith and trust shaken. Who could say what prompted her decisions? She must have thought them through carefully, because that's how Clara was. She wasn't impulsive.

What she wanted with all her heart was for it to be beneficial for all of them, and perhaps to her this was the way.

The family helped with the packing, and all was ready. Neighbors came to say good-bye. Some wished Clara "Good luck"; some cried. The children's friends said their good-byes in their own way—a hair ribbon, a pencil and tablet, ball and jacks, and for little Ben a metal horse and wagon. Then everyone left. Tomorrow was moving day.

That night as the youngsters got ready for bed, they questioned Slovie, "Why do we have to move? Where are we going?"

Slovie couldn't really answer. She had the same questions. She had always been able to talk with her mother about many things. But lately, Clara was usually upset and couldn't answer Slovie's questions. She looked at her younger sisters, wide-eyed, full of anxiety, and tried to console them.

"Don't worry," she tried to assure them. "We will all be together, won't we?"

They nodded and took comfort in that as they always did.

"Turn off the lights and let's go to bed."

There was silence for a few minutes; then Tobie asked wistfully, "Suie, are we ever coming back here?"

Thankful for the darkness, Slovie didn't answer right away. The lump in her throat was too big to swallow. Their situation didn't look too promising.

"I don't know. Maybe someday we will. We'll have to wait and see."

Slovie knew her sisters, too, hated to leave this house, their safe haven, and exchange it for the unknown.

They moved to the West Side.

In December, their baby sister, Sarah, was born and welcomed into the family. Everyone congratulated them, but Pa's grown son and daughter were not too happy. After all, he had become a grandfather and now here he was, the father of a new baby. His family was embarrassed. They had considered him an old man and couldn't handle the situation.

They were amicable in front of Pa and Clara and her family, but all the stealthy negativeness was said and done behind their backs. It came back to Clara, but she never talked against his family to anyone. To her that would have been disloyal. She busied herself caring for her family.

Chapter 30
The West Side

It was morning on the West Side, and the day began with a bright sun streaming in the opened windows. The neighborhood's youngsters were outdoors early and had already begun their busy day. Clara's children were playing ball and jacks on the cement steps out front, and across the street girls were playing hopscotch on chalk-marked sidewalks, while others were turning an old knotted rope, chanting, "One, two, buckle my shoe," and boys played ball in the street. All up and down State Street groups of children were seen doing the same.

There were no yards and there wasn't a blade of grass to be seen anywhere. The wooden porches of most of the houses sagged downward to meet the cracked sidewalks. The poor parched earth on the boulevards was packed down so hard that even the hardiest weeds had a difficult time breaking through its unyielding surface.

Here and there cottonwood trees managed miraculously to grow. When the plump seed pods burst open, fuzz balls wafted by slow winds were everywhere, sticking to everything, and a general nuisance from early spring through the summer.

The area was a settlement of mostly Jewish people, although Mexican, Irish, Lebanese, Syrians, and one black family lived there. This was a small, compact neighborhood with stores, businesses, homes, and synagogues that kept the Jewish community together. Most every household was struggling to make it through from day to day because of the hard economic times in the country.

The West Side was considered a very poor part of town to those not living there, but to those who did it was a most wonderful place where everybody belonged. Clara's children had no difficulty adjusting to it and made friends easily. They joined clubs at the Neighborhood House, a social gathering place for youngsters, and were kept busy with numerous educational activities with their peers, having fun, coming home content and happy.

The week passed quickly—for the children with school and play, for the fathers hard at work at their various jobs, and for the mothers kept busy caring for and nurturing their offspring. Then the whole Jewish community looked forward to Friday, when the bustling West

Side took on another life. All the Jewish shops closed before sundown and stayed closed until Saturday after sundown. Families went home to be together to participate ushering in the *Shabbos*.

After dinner, parents relaxed, and the children went out to visit friends or sit outdoors. Many just walked around the neighborhood, leisurely, strolling down the usually busy streets now hushed—at rest—for *Shabbos*.

Window curtains moved by slight summer breezes parted just enough so the lighted *Shabbos* candles in each home could be seen by those passing by. They brought a certain gladness to the heart, as they gave forth their brightening glow in the otherwise darkened homes.

A peace and calm descended everywhere: It was *Shabbos* on the West Side. The little community was carrying on the tradition of centuries past. It was observing the fourth biblical commandment: "Remember to keep the Sabbath holy."

On Saturday after lunch, many came out to sit on their porches. Porches were an integral part of life here. Neighbors and friends visited each other on the Sabbath to have a cup of tea with a piece of sponge cake or strudel. Porch sitters sometimes sat quietly watching the neighbors as they walked by or stopped to say hello. The porch sitters were observers of life on the West Side.

There were some porch sitters who thought they knew everything about everybody. If they drew their conclusions from outward appearances, they were wrong. They could never know what went on in the different homes. This was a neighborhood like others. There were many good things: businesses, people—good, hard-working people caring for their families.

But there was also a side not talked about here. It was unknown to some and ignored and overlooked by others, but it was the tragic side for the unfortunates who had to endure it.

On Saturday nights, but on other nights, too, some homes became gambling dens. Husbands and fathers who frequented them were served what the Prohibition law was against: bootlegged whiskey made in illicit stills in other homes and sold.

When the gamblers were so drunk they couldn't stand, their wallets were rifled of any money left, then they were brought home very late, dumped on the porches, and left to stagger into their homes. The drunkenness caused domestic quarrels, and the money that they could ill afford to lose added much to the family misery.

There were a few "ladies of the night," too, who had as their

172

steadies some of the husbands and fathers. The poor, suffering wives stayed home caring for their youngsters. In the morning, they came out to shop, trying to pretend all was well, but living their sad secret lives. They never complained; they endured the mental abuse and anguish. Sometimes they came out with large dark sunglasses to hide the evidence of physical abuse. There were households where sons were connected with mobsters and gangsters from Chicago and went to prison. Much of this spawned from the Prohibition era from 1920 to 1934. So many poor, law-abiding, hardworking parents couldn't understand and wouldn't believe how this could happen to their children, but the sad fact of life was, it did!

Still there was more good on the West Side to balance it all out.

Most of the West Side parents couldn't read or write English, having come from foreign countries where an education of any kind had been denied them because they were Jews. These hardworking parents felt it was important to give their children educational opportunities they never had. From their efforts, the West Side produced businessmen, doctors, lawyers, dentists, accountants, musicians, authors, teachers, nurses, and other successful men and women.

But then there were those who didn't see education as important, especially for girls. Pa Mintz was one of the latter. It may have been due to his upbringing in Russia, but from the first, when Clara's family moved to the West Side, he continually argued for the girls to quit school and go to work. Since they went to school every day, the subject of quitting became a constant, a cloud hanging over the household. It was difficult to cope with.

These incessant attacks on her children made Clara very unhappy. There was no reasoning with him, and it began to take its toll of her. At times, she became very stressed from Pa Mintz's perpetual outbursts about school and other things, and this fostered some very strong feelings in the children against their stepfather.

In the morning when he sat at the table, none of the children wanted to have breakfast. He sat scowling, ignoring anyone there. Slovie, being the oldest, led the way and sat down. The others followed. They sat, ill at ease, never lifting their eyes to look at him or each other. They ate very little and left hurriedly, feeling so stifled. They broke into a sigh of relief to be away from him.

They tried to deal with the problem in their own way. Somehow, they felt they were at fault. When they were going out, they never left without saying, "Good-bye, Mom! Good-bye, Pa!"

They stood at the opened door listening, hoping for a response.

173

Clara answered, but Pa Mintz never did. To her angry, disappointed siblings, Slovie said, "Never mind. We'll keep saying it anyway. It's the right thing to do."

In the hall, they separated to meet their friends. Slovie closed the door, feeling so downhearted that tears would start, and she would hurriedly wipe them away before opening the door to the outside. She walked out with a knot in her stomach, trying for the next few moments to regain her composure before meeting up with her school friends. She laughed with them, covering up the hurt that would gnaw at her the rest of the day.

Clara's family, for a long time, thought they were the only family that was a product of several marriages, having a stepfather, a stepsister, and different names. Then they met other families on the West Side who had their problems and worse. But they could only feel their own pain.

Every once in a while when the children were together playing or working, a supposedly friendly person, but a gossip nevertheless, would stop them and, like an inquisitor, ask pointed questions about their different surnames. Clara's children had been taught to be polite, so, squirming, they answered but felt very uncomfortable.

The children remembered Papa Max had been going to make them all Sugarmans, so on their own they went to school and changed their names to Mintz, and that put an end to the gossips' questions. Every now and then a new gossip would pick it up because Ben was still a Sugarman.

Clara didn't gossip and disliked gossipers. She believed that in God's eyes three people were hurt by gossip—first, the person the gossip was about; second, the gossiper; and third, the one listening to the gossip! All were diminished by it.

These attacks, unfair and untrue stories, were gossip that hurt people. No one knows what mean motives gossips have—ignorance, hate, jealousy, or plain maliciousness—but they have them, otherwise they wouldn't indulge in this cruel pastime.

When her children told her about the questions of their names, she became very angry. "It's too bad," Clara said, "people don't have better things to do. In a way people are cowards. They would never repeat the gossip face to face with their target. They do it furtively, behind their backs. The person isn't there to protect himself, which is wrong."

Clara's children heard her say many times, "If you hear people gossiping, don't enter into it."

Her children grew up with that; the lesson did remain with some of them. They were brought up to respect what was right.

Clara's children, though young, understood their circumstances. They couldn't do much about it, so they "behaved" as Slovie had told them, to avoid any trouble that might create a new problem. They never told anyone but kept it to themselves, hidden. It was a private matter, a weighty enigma. No matter what Pa Mintz said or did, they were very respectful of him. They did it for their mother! In their way, they analyzed the situation; at times it saved her from some troublesome predicaments.

They searched for answers. "Why is he angry all the time?"

Sometimes when things got really troublesome and one of them got an excessively abusive verbal treatment, they would discuss it among themselves, their support system. Slovie told them, "Think of Papa Max. He would never do that to you; it isn't you or your fault, so remember that!"

At school, Slovie studied hard. She cherished a private dream of going on to college but knew it was impossible. Pa Mintz was doing all he could to force her to quit high school, so how could she think of college? Slovie, knowing this, had signed up for a secretarial course, to prepare herself for work.

She loved school. Asking her to quit was like taking her life's blood from her. School was her saving grace. At school she forgot her problems at home.

One day Miss Fanning, Slovie's American history and homeroom teacher, asked her to stay after school. She wanted to know why Slovie was in secretarial instead of in college preparatory. Slovie told her she couldn't go to college and had to get a job after graduation.

Miss Fanning listened, then surprised the girl with, "I would like to send you to the college at Saint Cloud. I will pay your tuition for four years. All it will cost your parents is room and board."

Miss Fanning continued, "Do you think we can set up an appointment with your parents right away? Then we can change your curriculum so no more time is wasted." She was referring to the six weeks already gone by in the school term.

This was something Slovie had dreamed about, going to college; now here was a stranger offering her this incredible opportunity. "Why? Why would you do this for me, Miss Fanning?"

Miss Fanning explained, "Every few years I do this for a deserving student. This year I've chosen you."

Slovie must have looked bewildered, because she was. She didn't know how her teacher had arrived at her conclusion, but she thanked her over and over.

Slovie quickened her step homeward, her heart pounding, thinking of how this news would be met with at home.

Clara listened to the wonderful news, and her thoughts were of her daughter and how proud she was of her.

Clara had given all the money from the Busy Bee to Pa Mintz. She had never asked for anything for any of her children, but this was special.

That night when Clara broached the subject to him, it started a terrible quarrel. Slovie, pleading, promised that when she was through with school and got a job she would pay him back. But he wouldn't hear of it.

"No more school!" he thundered. "Let them go to work!"

Slovie had to face Miss Fanning the next morning. How do you explain to someone who is willing to do so much for you that you can't get the fifty dollars, even as a loan, from your family?

Miss Fanning sat back in her old swivel chair and took off her pince-nez. She closed her eyes for a minute, visibly disturbed, and looked very tired.

"Isn't there anyone who could help you with a loan?"

Slovie shook her head. "Who would do it for me? There is no one!" If Papa Max were here, she knew he would have helped her.

For days Slovie was furious with Pa Mintz. If he didn't want to help her, whatever his feelings, that was one thing, but she was tired of the constant "Quit school and go to work" routine. She wasn't hurting anyone, going to school.

Clara's family had suffered greatly for her to come here for freedom. Her children had the freedom of choice. They wanted an education, and here was Pa Mintz trying to deny them that. Clara was very angry that they had to take his abuse.

Slovie made up her mind she would never quit school until she graduated, no matter how much he tried to discourage her and her siblings.

It took a while to put her hopes and dreams aside. She attended school and did her best to get through. Miss Fanning remained a staunch friend. When she died, Slovie was very depressed and saddened. The world had lost a wonderful person who had wanted to do this extraordinary deed for her. Miss Fanning left Slovie a legacy, a legacy of high esteem, discipline, and feeling good about herself. Whatever she did in her life, she would remember this special teacher had touched her in so many positive ways.

Slovie got a Saturday job. With her hair put up and high heels on, she looked older. The person who hired her said she looked sophisticated and put her in the Millinery Department. The family had taken the scoldings about quitting school for three years. Slovie was fifteen.

Slovie brought home her first pay envelope with two precious dollar bills and thirty-eight cents in change in it. That was her Saturday's pay. It was the most money of her own she ever had in her whole life!

She couldn't believe her good fortune in landing the job. However, she had to stall the office for almost a year before she could bring her birth certificate to show she was sixteen. She didn't like not telling the truth, and it bothered her and worried her. The day she brought the certificate, a big load was lifted off her shoulders.

The money gave her a sense of independence. It wasn't much, but it would help her get through school. Spending carefully, it was enough for the few necessities. Clara still managed, once in a while, to sew some of their dresses. Slovie worked through summer and Christmas vacations and was able to help her sisters, sharing with them until they could get jobs.

So many times the pressure by Pa Mintz was so great, it would have been easier to do as he wanted. Slovie had discussed this with her mother. She felt guilty trying to go to school while her mother took the brunt of the bitter arguments, but Clara, a believer in education, urged Slovie to keep going and in this way gave her support.

Slovie felt if she quit, the others would, too, so she struggled through, doing her homework before Pa Mintz came home, so there would be no trouble. She felt it was important for her mother, her siblings, and herself. Later they would tell her, "You were always a good role model for us."

However, the pressure did affect Tobie, who quit after junior high school and got a job. No amount of talking to her could induce her to change her mind and go back to school. "I just can't take it anymore," she told her mother and sisters.

The Mintz household increased by one more, a son, Albert, named for Clara's brother, Avram.

Clara was busy raising the two smaller children. She was

happier now. The arguments about her children were not as frequent anymore. Pa Mintz had eased up on his temper outbursts, and the tension at home seemed to have abated, probably due to the fact that there were children of his own and the girls were working.

Life went along fairly smoothly now. They got along fine until something with Pa Mintz's family caused a disruption. The family needed a larger place. Clara and Pa Mintz discussed and agreed on different places to buy, but each time when it came to making the down payment, he changed his mind. Clara told him she knew that it was due to his family's interference, and he didn't deny it.

Clara got tired of the situation and finally gave up the idea of buying a house. It hurt, but she accepted what she couldn't change. They did find a bigger place and moved. The move came before the Passover holiday.

Clara, like the rest of the Jewish women, was preparing for the Passover dinner, which was a happy time for the family. The holiday celebrates the deliverance of our ancestors from slavery in Egypt, and at Passover families recall their roots.

Across the street, Slovie's friend was announcing, "Guess what? We're having company. My cousins are coming to dinner!"

An envious Slovie ran upstairs to talk to her mother, who was setting the table for the Passover seder.

"Why don't we ever have any relatives to invite for the holidays? Don't we have anybody? Why is that, Mom?" Slovie rattled off her angry spiel.

Slovie expected the answer she had heard her mother express other times: "Ich bien ellend vie a shtane [I am alone like a stone]." Instead, Clara answered, "You do have relatives!"

Slovie stopped her angry tirade, trying to comprehend the startling revelation she had just heard so matter-of-factly.

Her mother continued, "You have an aunt and uncle."

"I do?" Slovie asked in an incredulous tone. Why hadn't she heard this before? "Where? Where do they live?" She thought, *Far away, maybe in Europe.*

"Here!"

"Here? Where here?"

"Here in Minneapolis."

"Why don't we see them?"

"Do you want to see them?" Her mother seemed hesitant.

"Yes. What's their name?"

"Sadoff!" Just saying the name brought back memories to Clara,

178

memories that started tears. She and Liz hadn't spoken for many years, not since Clara's unhappy marriage to Liz's brother, Usher, ended in divorce. Clara used her apron to wipe the tears away. Heaving a deep sigh, she asked, "Would you like to talk to them? Call them. Look up the number in the phone book."

Slovie promptly picked up the book and started turning pages until she found "Sadoff." "There's a lot of them, Mom, a whole list of them!"

"Yes, I know. There are a lot of brothers."

"What's his first name?"

"Sol. Your uncle's first name is Sol!"

Slovie went down the list. "Michael, Morris, Sam, Sol. Here it is!" She couldn't believe this. Sol Sadoff was a real relative. "Shall I call?"

She picked up the phone, off its hook. "Number, please?" the operator asked.

Slovie gave her the number. She heard the phone ringing—once, twice. "I don't think anyone's home, Mom."

Then a woman's voice came on the line. "Hello? Hello?"

Slovie listened to the voice, a voice new to her, then asked, "Is this the Sadoffs'?"

"Yes. Who is this?"

Slovie handed the phone to her mother, then listened to this strange incident taking place.

"Hello, Lizzie?" She waited. "It's Clara."

Then there was silence on both sides of the line. Clara broke it by slowly asking, "How are you . . . and Sol . . . and the children?"

"Yes," Clara answered Lizzie's inquiry. "We're fine here, too." Clara explained the call, "Today Slovie asked me if we had any relatives. I told her yes. She wanted to talk to you, but I didn't know if you wanted to talk to her."

The hesitancy on both sides made it evident the situation was awkward for both of them. Clara continued, "I know you've been angry with me, but in all these years, you never tried to call or even see the children!"

Now there was a rising anger in her voice. This was something that hurt; her children were blameless. She handed the phone to Slovie. "Here's your Aunt Lizzie!"

"Hi!" Slovie didn't know what to say to this person, a stranger. To Slovie, at this moment, Clara and Liz's anger didn't matter to her. She had her own flesh-and-blood relative.

Her auntie asked about her sisters. "My sisters are outside."

Slovie wanted to talk about things important to her. Youngsters came right to the point. "Auntie, when am I going to see you?" Slovie wished she could see her now, today!

Her aunt told her, "After the holidays."

Clara took the phone and they wished each other, "Happy Passover," and said their good-byes.

Slovie's face wore a broad grin, a happy grin, as she put the receiver back on the phone hook. Lovingly, she stroked the black phone with her hand; it had brought her something she had longed for. "Mom! I have a real auntie! A real auntie!" Her voice was full of such joy.

"Don't get too excited," Clara cautioned. She didn't want Slovie disappointed.

Slovie ran down to tell her friend, "I just talked to my auntie!"

Her friend couldn't see what was so exciting about that. "So what? I talk to my auntie, too."

Slovie didn't explain to her friend. How do you explain what you don't understand? Her friend could never realize what this day meant to her.

That night Slovie went to bed and dreamed of Aunt Lizzie. She just saw her back and couldn't see her face. She thought about her the next day. What did she look like? She sounded nice. Was she?

Slovie, being the oldest, was there for her brothers and sisters. Her mother was busy now with the young brother and sister, and as Slovie grew older she needed someone close, a relative. She had wanted a relative, and now she had one. When would she see her?

In July Clara sent Slovie and Tobie to meet their aunt and uncle. The meeting was a little strange for all of them at first. The Sadoffs had two small sons, Melvin and Charlie, and Lizzie was pregnant with her third child, a daughter whom they would name Theresa. Later, another son, Leonard, was born.

Uncle Sol had a week's vacation from work. The family was going to a lake and took the girls with them. They spent a wonderful week at a cottage near Osseo, Minnesota. The girls had a chance to get to know their relatives, and the relatives had a chance to know the girls.

Tobie kept the boys busy swimming and playing in the lake and on the beach, and Slovie sat and talked to her aunt or helped her prepare some of the food. Her aunt said, "You must be a big help to your mother."

Slovie liked her. She was fair-faced and spoke softly, and Slovie

180

couldn't keep her eyes off of her. When she spoke, Slovie looked right at her, drinking in everything about her. Question after question she asked. Some were answered, and some were not. She wanted to learn in one week what she had missed all the years before.

Slovie liked her uncle Sol, too. He was a tall, thin, nice-looking man. His voice when he spoke to the girls was warm. They were both caring people.

Slovie observed their life, where children laughed, were happy— a nice family. This was something she and her siblings missed. She would have much to tell her mother.

Clara, busy raising her two youngsters, and Lizzie, raising hers, didn't have many opportunities to see each other, but Slovie visited her aunt and uncle on numerous occasions. They invited her to everything.

There developed a close relationship between Slovie and Aunt Lizzie's family. Slovie later stated, "She was the only relative I had. I needed her. She was someone for me to belong to."

Her Aunt Lizzie felt the same way. She had married into a big family, but they were Sol's family. Talking to Slovie, she said exactly what Clara had voiced: "Ich bien ellend vie a shtane [I am alone like a stone]. Now I have you. You're part of my brother and me! You're part of my life!"

They filled a need for each other. All of a sudden they were not alone!

It was a relationship important to both of them. An empty part of their lives, a void, was being partially filled.

Once Slovie asked her auntie if she could see a picture of her father. "I don't have one," Auntie Lizzie said. "Doesn't your mother have their wedding picture?"

"Yes, but she took my father off it!"

She could see her Auntie Lizzie becoming angry. Her face and neck reddened. "My picture," she explained, "got lost in the many movings." Then she changed the subject and wouldn't say anymore.

Slovie came home and studied her mother's wedding picture, her mother young and beautiful. What did her father look like in his wedding suit? Was he tall as her mother? Short?

I wonder if he was smiling, she thought. *Did he have happy lips or were they thin, stern lips? What was he really like?* She shook her head. She had a right to know but didn't. There was no mental image of him, and she would always wonder and never know.

Over the years Slovie asked many questions of Uncle Sol about her father. He would refuse to answer. "Ask your auntie," he would say. When she asked her auntie, she was told to ask her mother.

Each, Slovie thought, *tries to stay clear of any involvement through discussion.* Evidently it was something that pained them all!

Once Aunt Lizzie called Slovie. She wanted her to go to New York to help her find her father, Usher. This came as a shock to Slovie. Her auntie had never wanted to discuss him. *Why would she ask me now?* she wondered.

"I don't think I want to go, Auntie." She didn't want to hurt her but felt she was.

"He's your father. Don't you want to see him?" She seemed deeply offended.

"He was never a father to us, Auntie." It angered Slovie when she thought what the family had been going through, was still going through, because of him. "My mother would be very hurt, and she would be right. You never heard from him. Why do you want to find him now?"

Then Lizzie told her she had heard from him, quite a while ago. He had written her from New York, asking for financial help. She said Sol refused to give it to him and this had caused a serious rift in their relationship.

Slovie tried to ease her pain. "Times were hard, Auntie."

"No! No!" She was angry. "He just wouldn't help him!"

Her auntie pleaded with her, "I want to see him. Who knows how long I'll live? I want to see him!"

Slovie thought about it. She loved her auntie and was torn between these family members, angry with each other. Slovie and her aunt talked about it and it was decided her aunt would run ads in the New York Jewish newspapers.

"Auntie, as soon as you hear anything, let me know. I'll have to tell Mother." Slovie didn't want to be disloyal to her mother, but she wanted to help her aunt. "If it's all right with her, I'll go with you, Auntie."

Lizzie was very appreciative. "It means a lot to me that you want to do this for me."

The ads ran for a long time, but there was no response to them. Eventually Lizzie called Slovie to tell her she was not running them anymore. She sounded quite discouraged; she had counted on this to find him. It would have meant a great deal to her to see him, to talk to him.

Slovie tried to console her, "Auntie, you did try to find him."

In a sad voice, she murmured, "No, it was too late."

Clara had lived with the hurt her first husband had inflicted on her and the children, resulting in much hardship for them, changing their lives.

Aunt Liz was angry with Clara because she hadn't taken Usher back, and was sad and bitter because she couldn't help him when asked for it, and blamed Sol.

Sol was angry because of the rift this caused between him and Lizzie, a situation never completely resolved.

For many years Slovie had put questions to them that went unanswered. They went to their graves with whatever they wouldn't talk about—all thinking of their own feelings, never realizing they left Slovie here with hers, wondering.

Chapter 31

Life after School

"Something wonderful is happening tonight," Clara told her friends. They all knew it was of great importance to her; she brought it up whenever she saw them. They were good friends and shared her happiness.

Tonight Clara was going with Slovie to shop for a graduation dress. What made it all the more wonderful was the opportunity it afforded them to be together, just the two of them.

They left after dinner and were crossing the Robert Street Bridge on their way to the Golden Rule, one of the fine department stores in Saint Paul.

Clara began the conversation, "I'm so proud of you, Slovie."

Many nights she prayed for life to be easier for her daughter. She was sure with a high school education it would be, and now Slovie's perseverance had brought them to this wonderful day.

They hurried on, not wanting to miss anything of what the evening had in store. They found the seats with the help of an usherette, and then it began—the style show. It was the first one Clara or Slovie had ever seen, and to them it was magical.

The models were lovely in the different styles in spring pastel colors. The rapt audience sat wide-eyed, full of wonder, enjoying this fantasy world.

When it was over, everyone asked, "Wasn't it just too wonderful?"

"Slovie, which one did you like?" one girl asked.

They were all so beautiful, but without hesitation, Slovie pointed out the precious dress in pink silk net. "I like that one!"

"Me, too!" Her mother wholeheartedly agreed with Slovie's choice. Slovie went to try it on while her mother waited, watching the other girls and their mothers.

When Slovie came out, Clara gasped, "You look so beautiful!"

It was the same sentiment voiced by other mothers of the graduates, seeing their daughters so grown-up—young ladies in these lovely long gowns.

The girls looked at themselves in the mirrors, then primped this way and that. Overnight they seemed to have crossed over from girlhood to young womanhood and surprised everyone, including themselves.

Slovie hadn't had much time to scrutinize herself. Now, she went close to the mirror and touched her long brown hair with a blond streak on the right side. Her eyes, she observed, were green with gold-brown specks, and she had freckles on her nose. She wasn't too tall, about five feet, four inches, and was thin. There wasn't an outstanding, special thing about her that she could see. One of her friends looked like Norma Shearer, the beautiful actress. Slovie just looked like, well, Slovie.

Her mother once told her everyone is different, unique in their own way. She had told Slovie she was beautiful, but that was her mother. All mothers say that!

Early on Slovie came to this conclusion, *I can't be anyone but me, so I'll be satisfied with me!* She accepted herself.

On the way home they talked about the style show and how beautiful everyone looked. They stopped at Finn's Drugstore. "Come; we'll have a little ice cream," Clara said as she opened the door.

"Are you sure, Mom?"

"I'm sure." After all, this was a special night for the two of them.

Lou Finn, the proprietor, came up. "Hi, Mrs. Mintz. Hi, Slovie. What will you ladies have?"

They ordered two chocolate sundaes. While they waited, Clara spoke up. "Slovie, we don't get to talk too much." Clara, busy with young Sarah and Al, not even a year old, knew she hadn't been able to spend much time with her older ones. They were busy with work and school, at home did what they could to help her, and were busy some evenings with friends. Caring for the younger ones and the house, and Pa, kept Clara busy and tired, but the children understood.

Slovie looked at her mother. There were a lot of gray hairs mixing with the brown. Clara looked tired and serious.

"Sometimes at night before I fall asleep, I think of my children," Clara went on. "I think of you, Slovie. From the time you were little you helped me with everything. For a young person, you always understood how things were. You never gave me any trouble. You never blamed me for anything." Clara's voice was faltering, and she couldn't go on.

Lou Finn brought the sundaes and walked away. He could see they were in serious conversation.

"That's all right, Mom. You don't have to talk about it." Slovie took a spoonful of the sundae.

185

"Yes, I have to talk about it. It was hard for you and it hurt me many times to see how much you had to do, but like a *mamaleh* you did it. So many times I asked God to bless you, to make your life good!"

Slovie's eyes met her mother's as she spoke almost apologetically. "Mom, sometimes I wasn't so good. I would get very angry and go into the bathroom or bedroom so no one would see me. I was angry with you; then I'd get upset with me for being angry with you. Other times I was angry with the kids; then I'd get upset with me again for that. Most of the time I was upset with me. I wanted things to be better for all of us and couldn't change anything, and that was hard to accept."

"Bist dach a shtarkeh mensh, Sloveleh [you are a strong person, Slovie]."

"If I am, I learned from you, Mom. I have you to thank for that and a lot of other things, too. You were always there for us. You always cared, Mom."

There was a strong bond between these two.

Clara continued, "I don't say it enough and I want you to know, and never forget, how much I love you. I wish I could have given you more."

Slovie reached across the table, putting her hand over her mother's. She was deeply touched. "I don't say it often either; you know I love you, Mom."

Then both were silent, finishing up the melting sundaes, thinking their own thoughts. Slovie's mother's head was bent, and Slovie knew she was crying. She handed her another paper napkin and thought, *My mother, since I can remember, has had so many things to cry about. She had so much pain, went through so much, and through it all was such a wonderful person.*

She hoped she could be like her. Her mother was a good person.

Slovie was glad they had that chance to talk together. She had missed this with her mother and told her so, but their lives, for a long time, had not been conducive to revealing their feelings.

Clara felt better, too. It seemed raising her children had taken a long time, but it really hadn't. Here, now, was Slovie, soon ready to go out into the world, and it frightened her.

They finished their sundaes and sat awhile longer, discussing the last days of school. "Everyone says they are glad school is over, but I'll miss it, Mom."

When they got up, Slovie said, "Thanks, Mom."

"Oh, the sundae is nothing."

186

"No, for talking to me."

Outside, they hugged each other and started home.

Slovie's sisters were waiting to hear about the show. "Where's your dress?"

Slovie explained it was ordered and they would see it in a few weeks. "Wait 'til you see it!"

That night before she fell asleep, Slovie retraced the evening's events—the breathtaking style show, the beautiful dress she chose—but most of all, she was so happy to have had the opportunity to talk with her mother. Those moments were rare, not coming often, and she treasured them. They were an important part of her growing up.

A week before graduation, the dress arrived. When Slovie came home, she found her mother had pressed and hung it. All that week Clara invited neighbors to come in to see it. She had everybody excited about her daughter's graduation.

Graduation night, Slovie's sisters watched her get dressed.

"It's so pretty. Can we try it on tomorrow?"

"Sure, tomorrow you can put it on."

"With your high heels?"

"Yes," she assured them, and they couldn't wait.

Clara watched, with so many feelings spilling over in her—gladness, sadness, and pride—and now repeated what she had so often said: "Oh, if my mother could only have seen you, it would have brought her such *nachis* [happiness]."

Graduation for Humboldt High School was held in the big auditorium in downtown Saint Paul on a warm June night in 1931.

Clara came with Pa Mintz, who had mellowed out considerably. Tobie and Ben came to help them find their way. Rosie stayed home with Sarah and Baby Al, and Aunt Lizzie and Uncle Sol attended graduation, too.

The auditorium was packed and very warm. All through the audience the programs listing the graduation exercises were highly visible—doubling as fans, waved to and fro. They were not very successful in trying to manufacture even slight movements in the hot, humid air.

It was almost time to begin, but as at all functions, the late-comers were rushing around to find their seats. The instruments in the orchestra were being sounded, and every once in a while the blare of a trumpet or the roll of a kettledrum could be heard.

The lights dimmed and the noisy audience began to quiet down. The orchestra began to play "Pomp and Circumstance," and heads turned to see the graduates coming down the aisles—lovely girls in their gowns on one side and handsome young men in their white flannel trousers and navy jackets on the other. They marched up onstage, taking their assigned seats.

Slovie saw her mother wave her handkerchief; she glanced at her for barely a second, worried not to misstep. The graduates stood until everyone was onstage, then sat down in unison. They made a lovely picture. It was a wondrous sight for the proud parents and loved ones watching—a once-in-a-lifetime thrill for them all!

A dream of Clara's had come true. "You're the oldest, *Sloveleh*," she had said to her daughter, "and, God willing, I will see the first of many good things through you."

After the graduation exercises, Slovie and a few of her friends walked through the downtown, then across the good old Robert Street Bridge. The new white high heels caused blistered heels and pinched toes and were taken off.

The girls looked up at the vast midnight blue sky and saw millions of stars, and here they were, after a four-year struggle, finally having reached an important goal in their lives.

They stopped in the middle of the bridge, a favorite stopping point, and as they looked down at some boats passing by, they voiced their wishes and dreams.

"I wish I were on that boat going far away," one friend announced.

"I wish I had a steady boyfriend so I could get married," another said. She didn't want to worry about finding a job.

Slovie silently wished she could have gone on to college at Saint Cloud, but since that wasn't to be, she would accept the situation. It was one she couldn't change.

Out loud she joined her friends with, "I wish I find a good job soon."

The following week, with a résumé that included a recommendation from her shorthand teacher, Mrs. Ryan, she began her job hunting, calling on offices in one building after another, trying to get a secretarial position. Some offices were pleasant enough to let her fill out an application, which made her hopeful. Others were not so accommodating, and some people were rude. Some sounded enthusiastic and would call her. She came home feeling very optimistic, sure something from one of the offices would turn out for her—maybe even tomorrow or next week!

Every day she had to endure Pa Mintz's taunts. "So she went to school and can't find a job. And Tobie, who didn't go to school, got a job!"

According to him, Slovie had wasted her time when she could have made money. It was pretty difficult not to be disrespectful and answer back. She bit her lip and had to listen. This was something that she had to face every day until she found a job.

When a few months had gone by, she did become greatly concerned. She needed the job desperately. She had hoped for one where she could use the skills she had learned for four years—bookkeeping, taking dictation in shorthand, and typing. This had been of the utmost importance to her, but she now realized she might not find one.

There were so many people unemployed in 1931 that she felt lucky to have her part-time job in the Millinery Department, but there was little chance for full-time work. Yetta, the young woman who was manager of the department, would probably be there for years.

Slovie prayed for help in finding full-time employment. Prayers are answered in mysterious ways, and no one would have imagined that it would take the U.S. Navy to answer Slovie's prayers, but it did.

Mr. Klein, manager of the store, called Slovie in at noon that Saturday. She was very nervous and hoped she wasn't getting fired. People were getting cut from many departments.

With a palpitating heart, she entered the office, his inner sanctum, and watched Mr. Klein's face as he sat at his desk. There wasn't an inkling of what he wanted of her. He asked her to be seated; then while she waited, he looked through her file. (She had seen her name on it.)

Slowly, he closed it. When he looked up, he astounded her with, "We are losing Miss Yetta, and she has recommended you to take over the department. It's quite a responsibility. Would you be interested?"

She was so relieved she wasn't getting fired. She was a little dazed, too. It wasn't what she had been looking for, but "a bird in the hand is worth two in the bush."

"Well?" He waited. "You have a little time to think about it, only Miss Yetta would like to leave in two weeks."

"Thank you. I'll be happy to take it and I'll do my best!"

"I know you will. That's why we've considered you." He was actually smiling as he shook her hand.

Slovie almost stumbled down the steps from his office and hurried to speak to Yetta.

Yetta looked at Slovie. "Did you take the job?"

Slovie nodded her head up and down. She couldn't talk, she was so overwhelmed.

"Good, you'll do a good job." Yetta assured her.

"I'm leaving to be married to Goody." Yetta had always talked about her boyfriend, Goody, but had never said what he did. Now she said, "Goody is a Jewish chaplain in the navy, and has been called to duty in Florida."

"Why?" They didn't know, but those in charge knew—war clouds were slowly gathering.

"We're going to be married in a few weeks." Yetta was so excited and happy, and Slovie was happy for her and congratulated her, "Mazel tov!"

Slovie couldn't wait to tell her mother. To her mother she confided, "I'm a little frightened. There's a lot to learn and it's a challenge, but I'm going to learn all I can about this job!"

It proved to be a wonderfully creative experience, besides a wonderful learning experience in running a small business, since the department was franchised out of Chicago. She learned how to make hats, working on wool felt in winter and lovely straws in summer. It was exciting to create your own product for customers. There was a great sense of satisfaction and accomplishment in running the department, so it was profitable.

Slovie gave credit to Clara, her mother, saying, "I think we all inherited the creativity from her, but in different ways."

Working in the store during the summer was tough. There were very few ceiling fans; the doors were left open to encourage customers to walk in, but this also let in more of the heat from the broiling sun. At the end of the day everyone was exhausted.

Sometimes the girls met some of their friends at Cordelli's Drugstore for a cool, refreshing phosphate or Coke before tackling the walk home across the bridge. Tired as they were, they wore their high heels and wouldn't dare wear comfortable low heels, just in case some of the boys came by. They suffered, all for vanity's sake.

They got home, after bravely smiling their way through those already sitting on their porches, then dashed into the hallways to throw off the high heels and breathe a sigh of relief.

Slovie and her friends always had a wonderful summer. The boys rented a cottage at Wildwood, White Bear Lake, from June through October. The girls rented theirs from June through August. They chipped in fifteen dollars apiece and for seventy-five dollars and sharing food, they had a full summer of entertainment.

Living at Wildwood was somewhat primitive, with the outhouses in back quite far from the cottages. At least two girls got up to accompany the one in need of the facility. There was always one braver than the rest who led the foray through the bushes and trees. They were frightened and carried flashlights, and one always took the old, dilapidated broom "just in case someone is out there."

Some cottages had porches with wooden swings, and beds wherever one could be set up. The kitchens had wooden tables with a miscellaneous collection of chairs, and the infernal water pumps in the sinks wore out one's arms trying to pump up even one glass of water!

The iceboxes simply devoured the large blocks of ice brought in two and sometimes three times a week, and the outhouse got a lot of soured milk and spoiled food!

There was always someone from a cottage driving out to the lake every night after work. Those who could go got a ride. Most everyone came out on the weekend, so beaches were crowded.

Everything was within walking distance—the dance hall and refreshment stands where the boys bought Cokes for their girls. At night, they sat in pairs, arms around each other, on old tree trunks—some near the beach, others away from it—watching the sun sink down the horizon into the lake.

Sometimes they went to the Wildwood Dance Hall for part of the evening, then came back, and all helped to get a fire going on the beach, prepare hot dogs and buns, and toast marshmallows.

Once, one smarty brought a small flask with liquor to spike the Cokes. It wasn't appreciated by the girls, and the boys never tried it again.

All the boys and girls of this group came from poor, hardworking families and didn't have much money to spend, but they spent wisely when they invested in the cottages for the summer. The weekends, especially Saturday nights, were happy times with good, clean fun!

At the lake during the day, if one was on vacation or not working, there were other simple, enjoyable things to do. Sometimes Slovie and her friends would sit with fishing poles just watching the birds in the sky, lost in thought, lazily gazing at the different shades of green of trees and brush across the lake or along the shore, quietly reflecting. Once in a while they surprised even themselves, when they actually caught some fish and fixed a delicious lunch or dinner.

There were other days, too, where Slovie and a friend sprawled on a blanket, sometimes in the sun, sometimes in the shade, together—not talking—reading for hours, lost in the different worlds in their books. So many faraway places to read about and dream about. She so admired the people who had written these books that gave her so much pleasure.

Those wonderful days of summer gave Slovie time to learn about herself, to know herself through hours of quiet reflection she so enjoyed. There were things she liked about herself and some things she didn't. She knew she wasn't perfect! She was content to a point, but there was discontent, too. There were her dreams!

She thought about her sisters—they were close to her. She thought about her brother Ben—a nice boy, almost nine. Pa Mintz was demanding much from a nine-year-old who came every day after school for the monotonous job of dusting boxes and running errands.

She thought about young Sarah, almost six years old, and Baby Albert. It was a wonderful family, and Slovie could see where the events of the past few years had left their mark, causing some to grow up with insecurities and others to strengthen. Her thoughts were of her wonderful mother who as she grew older worked harder, happy caring for her family.

Life moved along for their family on the West Side—arm in arm it marched with time.

Chapter 32

The Intervening Years!

Clara's daughters, all grown-up, were working now and helped her in any way they could. They were all very personable, well-liked, popular young ladies and were invited to all the important Jewish social functions.

The dates were usually dinner out at the Lowry or Saint Paul Hotel, with dancing in the fabulous ballrooms with their spectacular crystal chandeliers. Big-name bands such as Tommy Dorseys's, Guy Lombardo's, Harry James's and so many others played their wonderful music, tunes that kept whirling around in the brain a long time after the dance was over.

Slovie would come home and tell her mother about the wonderful evening—how exciting it was when the doorman opened the doors for them, and about walking through the beautifully carpeted lobby to the elevator, trimmed in gold, that took them up to the dining room. She would describe all the details, including some of the beautifully dressed women she met, and in this way let her mother share and enjoy all these wonderful things with her.

The girls wore formals. Slovie and Tobie had one each and took turns wearing them. The young men didn't have cars, so travel was by streetcar and once in a while by taxi.

Late at night coming home, they would walk arm in arm and stop on the old Robert Street Bridge, observing the boats on the Mississippi River, or listen to the music drifting up from river steamboats anchored at their wharves below.

The twin arched bridge was a lovely old stone one that silently gathered to its bosom a bit of the life of all those who crossed it. It couldn't tell the bad or the good of those who tarried on it, or what the star-struck lovers said to each other, or even give a hint of the dreams and hopes of the eager, restless youth. It just stood there for years, patiently waiting, watching, and listening!

Sometimes the girls double-dated. One of Slovie's dates brought a friend for Tobie. Most of the young men were pretty well-behaved, but every once in a while there would be a new one with "wandering hands." When that happened, there was naturally a sisterly concern for each other. The girls had a signal prearranged that warned the

193

other there was a little trouble. The pursued girl would put on an act worthy of an Academy Award. It usually began with, "Oh, I'm so sick." She would double over as if in great pain. "Quick, I'd better get out. I think I'm going to throw up."

The co-conspirator would sound so anguished. "Oh, you poor thing! Hurry, I'll take you upstairs."

The men worked hard and long to purchase cars. Sometimes two fellows went in partnership to own one. They cared for it as if it were the Hope diamond, so it wasn't difficult to understand that they didn't want anyone messing it up. Out they would scramble, so the girls could quickly leave. The girls said their good-byes and ran in. Then, safe in the dark hallway, they watched as the boys, grumbling, rode off. The girls would sit on the stairs, stifling their giggles and laughter, happy to have gotten rid of the young man who wouldn't stop but kept maneuvering his two hands like the tentacles of an octopus.

The time was in the 1930s, still the Prohibition era. From the 1920s on girls were being seen on the silver screen smoking, drinking out of special little flasks carried in purses, wearing tight, short-short dresses, rolled hose, and dancing the "wild" dances like the Charleston and the Shimmy Shake, and others.

Promiscuity was also shown in the movies, and a furor arose around the country, and fear, fear the young people were beginning to pick up these ideas. There was worry that the younger generation was "going to the devil."

There were many who did not follow, who remained true to the old-fashioned values, and the Mintz girls were among those.

The dates were narrowing down to one or two boys for Slovie that were pretty steady. Neighbors had their bets on which one it would be. She took their kidding good-naturedly but said nothing. What could she say? She didn't feel ready to commit herself yet. True, they were nice young men from nice families, but she felt she was too young and had not been out in the world enough. She was only twenty!

Clara and Pa Mintz thought it was indeed time. The consensus was that girls not married before twenty-two were on the way to becoming "old maids." Again Slovie was reminded that she was the oldest. They were all waiting. She shrugged off their pressure and wouldn't be hurried.

The other sisters were dating, too. Tobie had some boyfriends, but no one special yet. Rosie and her friends, the younger crowd, went on dates. They loved dancing and usually went down to the river steamboats, where they had wonderful music.

It was on a weekend in 1934 that two Jewish organizations—Hadassah for young women and B'Nai B'Rith for young men—were having a co-sponsored regional convention in Duluth, Minnesota. Slovie, a member of Hadassah, was planning to attend with a friend. She thought, *It'll be nice, a change, to get away and see Duluth.* She had heard so much about it: the big lake, the drive along North Shore, and the lighthouse high on a rock. It all sounded so wonderful. She had never been that far out of the Twin Cities. The more she thought about it, the more exciting the trip became!

At the bus depot, there were so many young women greeting friends and trying to keep track of luggage, while the bus drivers were frantically attempting to get the chattering females on their buses so they could leave on time.

The ride up was fun—relaxing for those who were "nervous Tillies"; singing and joking and laughter for those committed to having a good time—then it ended when they got off at Hinckley and stopped at Tobie's Cafe, famous for its enormous caramel rolls. The rest of the ride up was hilarious, and they arrived at Hotel Duluth pretty tired out and full of expectations!

The young women registered, then were anxious to get out and walk around to see the sights. Slovie and a friend walked down the block to Lake Superior. They had never seen a lake this large, the largest of the Great Lakes. They looked out and saw a few boats off in the distance. They sat on a rock and watched the sun as it shimmered on the water. Slovie loved the water; it was so calming, so soothing. Reluctantly they got up and started back.

There was a message inviting them to *Shabbos* dinner at the home of the Apple family, relatives of Slovie's friend's sister-in-law. Slovie was hesitant about going, since she didn't know the family and felt it was an imposition, but her friend assured her they were both invited. They barely had time to catch a taxi and make it to the Apples'.

The girls were greeted royally, and Slovie met the parents, their two sons, Bill, in high school, and Sam, who had just come in from work. Then there was an Uncle Sam who had come down to Saint Paul and dated Slovie's friend on occasion. They were a warm, outgoing family. The stranger was welcomed to share in the *Shabbat* that tied them together as Jews, and they were strangers no more.

The dinner was a huge success, and everyone was in an exceptionally good mood. After dinner they sat out on the back porch. It was a lovely sight looking down the hill to the lake. Duluth is a city built on a hill about a mile high.

The two Sams took the girls for a drive up along North Shore so they could see the sights. The boys were very gracious about it, but they must have gotten pretty bored having to take all their visitors up along the same route.

The boys stopped at the famous lift-bridge. Duluth is a large harbor for ore barges, so it was a learning experience when the girls heard the whistles of the ore boats off in the distance giving their warning that they were approaching, so the bridge could be raised to let them through. The girls watched as the bridge lifted and the ore barges went slowly gliding by, lights twinkling on the boats, and listened to the sound of voices of people aboard.

Slovie's friend and Uncle Sam hadn't seen each other for a while, so were deeply engrossed in each other. The other, Sam Apple, kept asking Slovie questions about herself. Then he surprised her by saying he had seen her two years before on a visit to a cousin in Saint Paul. He had wanted to meet her then but was told she had a steady boyfriend. He said it almost as a question, as if he was interested in knowing what the status of that situation was now.

She caught that and answered, "I do have many friends."

"What about tomorrow night?" he asked. "Will you go to the dance with me?"

Slovie had been listening carefully to him. He had sounded so sincere and impressed her with his earnestness and enthusiasm as he spoke of opening his own small business, an advertising company called the Duluth Display Service. He was very proud of it, struggling with very little money, but he was optimistic and very hopeful.

She accepted his date for the dance.

Later, back at the hotel, her thoughts were of him. She had never met anyone quite like him. Of course, he was eight years older, and that may have made the difference. He had his feet on the ground, and she admired his courage, because that was what it took to make a beginning—courage plus hard work. He was a very likable chap.

Her friend interrupted her thoughts, "Well, how did you like Sam Apple?"

"Nice. He's very nice!"

On Saturday, after the dinner, speeches, and awards, all headed for the ballroom. The boys and men were lined up like nervous stallions, chomping at the bits, looking the girls over as they entered. The girls, eager, hoped they would be asked to dance, not wanting to suffer the embarrassment of "wallflower" status.

Slovie wore a peach satin formal with rhinestone straps. Sam Apple had been watching for her and practically elbowed his way through the throng to her, afraid someone else would beat him there. He held her arm tightly as he led her to the dance floor, and soon they were dancing in a fenced-in enclosure on the floor.

Several young men cut in, and Sam introduced her. In order to get on the dance floor they had to purchase tickets. One young man who cut in had a long string of tickets and wouldn't let Slovie go. Sam motioned her to come out, but she had to stay until the tickets were used up, as the dance was for the charities.

Slovie and Sam left the dance floor when he saw too many buying tickets to dance with her. The evening was a huge success, and so was the convention. The girls heard later there were many marriages resulting from the affair!

The two Sams, after much persuasion, finally induced the girls into staying another day. The boys drove them to the bus, and Sam Apple gave Slovie a big box of chocolates and wanted to know if he could come down the next week. He let her know he was serious about her.

"You can come," she told him, "but I'm not committing myself to anything."

"Fair enough," he said, happy she would see him.

Slovie couldn't say what this persistent young man wanted to hear. She had just met him. How could she say she loved him? She was very honest with him. "We'll have to wait and see," she told him.

He knew he was in love with her and had been since the first time he had seen her.

He stepped up on the bus, visibly concerned because she was leaving. Softly he spoke to her. He wanted to kiss her.

"Right here in front of everybody?"

"Yes," he said, looking so serious. "I won't see you for a while."

The noise on the bus was slowly diminishing as people became aware of something out of the ordinary taking place at the front of the vehicle. Slovie knew there were many eyes on them and she was a private person, but nothing would dissuade Sam.

He kissed her and the whole bus cheered and applauded and whistled.

The bus started up and she saw him waving, running on the sidewalk. People were shouting, "Be careful! Be careful!"

All the way home, Slovie's friend extolled Uncle Sam's virtues.

Slovie listened and didn't say anything, but she thought about the turn of events this past weekend. She was flattered, as any young girl would be, at all the obviously sincere attention by Sam. What would it mean to her, to her life? Maybe something; then again, perhaps nothing! Who could tell? Soon she would be home and life would resume its normalcy.

At home Clara questioned. "What happened in Duluth?"

Slovie told her about the convention, the dance, and dinner at the Apples' and added, "Nothing else, Mom."

One night during the week there was a knock, a very loud knock, on the door. Somebody seemed to be in a hurry. Clara answered the door.

"Slovie, come here and sign this!"

Everyone came running to see what was happening. Clara was holding a long box.

"What is it?" the younger ones wanted to know. Slovie opened the box and found beautiful long-stemmed roses.

"Who sent them?" they clamored. Slovie was taking the card from the envelope and began reading, and her face reddened.

To the most beautiful girl in the world.
                                    Love,
                                    Sam Apple

Slovie knew she wasn't the most beautiful girl in the world, but beauty is in the eyes of the beholder. Today, his card made her feel special.

They put the roses in a tall vase borrowed from upstairs and put it on the dining room table. The family and neighbors from upstairs stood admiring them, the younger ones smelling and touching them.

"Who's Sam Apple?" Clara wanted to know. This was all wonderful, but she had questions! "Roses from someone you just met?" She wondered what that could mean.

Slovie couldn't contain her excitement. With her face flushed she looked at her mother. "Mom," she blurted, "this is another first!"

Word spread through the West Side by the younger sisters and brothers and their friends. Everyone was excited. There was much discussion. After all, sending flowers was, indeed, serious business!

Sam sent special delivery letters and roses, and the telephone wires between Duluth and Saint Paul hummed with his love messages. He came down on Saturday nights when he could, and soon he and Slovie were talking of their future together.

On Hanukkah he gave her a lovely ring and they were officially engaged. The whole West Side buzzed with the engagement. Everyone was happy for Slovie and the Mintzes. They heard Sam was a nice young chap and "in business."

Sam came down in early spring, and they picked out their bedroom and living room furniture. In May the bride-to-be came up to Duluth and they rented a two-room apartment and fixed it up with their furniture and things. They made a lovely little home, a place of their own. They were two very happy people. When everything was ready, they shut the door, and they wouldn't enter the apartment again until after they were married.

On June 7, 1936, their wedding day arrived, the day they had been waiting for. Two of Slovie's friends and Tobie and Rosie were bridesmaids. Little Al was ring bearer and Pa Mintz's granddaughter, the child of his daughter, was flower girl. Ben was in charge of ushering and handling any problems in the synagogue.

The night before the wedding, Slovie had stayed up late to talk to Pa Mintz. Simply, she thanked him "for everything." Pa Mintz had never been a demonstrative person. She had never seen him kiss or hug his own children, but his eyes misted up and she gently kissed him on the forehead. She got up to go. "Good night, Pa." He surprised her with "Good night Slovie." She swallowed the lump in her throat; she had waited so long to hear that. She went to bed as thoughts of the happenings of the past ten years kaleidoscoped through her mind. Some passed quickly; others stayed—some she would forget; some she would remember. One thing she always knew—how much she loved her family and how much they meant to her.

Everyone said the bride and groom were a very handsome couple, but isn't that true of every bridal couple? The photographer came and took the pictures of the wonderful group. Wedding pictures are important. They are a pictorial record of a very special day, a day uniting two young people in love, setting them forth on their life's journey together—full of hope and faith and promise. So it was with Slovie and Sam!

The wedding day was bright and sunny. "A good omen," they said. "Happy the bride the sun shines on!"

The wedding took place in the synagogue, and they were married by two rabbis, one Orthodox and one Conservative.

The wedding of her daughter was another first for Clara. She shed tears of happiness and sadness, too. She prayed for life to be good to her child. Everyone was happy. Pa Mintz smiled all that day!

Slovie was happy, but marriage was taking her away from those she loved at home. She would miss them. That night saying good-bye was difficult. Her siblings promised her they would be good to each other, and she promised, "Don't worry. I'll come to see you."

Sam, seeing her distress, said they would come down as often as they could.

"I'll write. Remember, I love you."

They all tried bravely to hide the tears as they hugged her.

The newlywed Apples moved to Duluth, and Sam was busy with his display service. The new bride got a part-time job in a small department store owned by one of Sam's uncles.

The couple made friends and were happy in their little two-room apartment. Sam came home for dinner usually bringing a token of his affection. One day he brought a kitchen stool she needed. He had painted "Sweet Slovie" on it.

Every once in a while he brought a single beautiful rose, and one day he showed her two lovely little red intertwining hearts with "Slovie and Sam" painted on them, and she, no poet, but in love, wrote poetry to him and later added to it.

Wonderful, Wonderful You
by Slovie Apple

I

When we were young our love was new,
And stopped for us was time.
My heart filled with song
To think I belonged to wonderful, wonderful you.

II

Our days were canopied skies of blue;
Our nights were star-filled forevers.
My heart filled with song
To think I belonged to wonderful, wonderful you.

200

Over lush green meadows we wandered, we two
And danced on fields of clover.
My heart filled with song
To think I belonged to wonderful, wonderful you.

Slovie wrote long letters home that made her mother happy, and the Apples did come down Saturday nights and go back on Sunday. Pa Mintz, who didn't say much to anybody, liked Sam and sat and talked to him about business and other things. The others sat near their newly married sister, talking to her, little Al on her lap.

The situation at home seemed to be improving. Every summer Pa Mintz rented a cottage at White Bear Lake for Clara and the two younger children. Ben, almost fourteen, worked in the store after school and on Sundays and summer vacations.

Clara had begun English classes at the Neighborhood House. The classes were held after dinner, and she was so proud as she carried her reader to school. She was anxious to learn, to pass her tests for her citizenship papers. This included knowing the presidents of the United States, certain amendments to the Constitution, and struggling through with her reading. She was doing great, and was so motivated, but Pa Mintz's mind about education for women hadn't changed and he was not supportive of her. This was really too bad, for she was a good student.

The Apples were adjusting to married life that first year and the following year had their first child, a daughter, Darlene (Devorah in Hebrew), named for Sam's maternal grandmother, and Clara's first grandchild.

The following year the Apples presented Clara with her first grandson, Martin (Mordecai in Hebrew), named for Clara's grandfather.

The next year Tobie eloped with Jerome Blumenthal, a young man she met at work. Rosie was her witness. The newlyweds each went back to their homes, afraid to tell their folks they were married, but eventually they had to, and the couple went to live with Jerome's parents. Tobie and Jerome had two sons, Steven and Eugene.

Rosie married her young man, Clayton Rein, whom she had been going with since early school days. From that union came three children: Judy, Burton, and Stanley.

Ben graduated from high school in 1940 and started the

University of Minnesota pre-law classes. He worked long hours in the store and tried to do his homework, but soon Pa Mintz began the scoldings if Ben brought his books to the store, so he studied only in between customers.

Ben came to see Slovie and Sam and discussed leaving school. She pleaded with him to continue, but he had to make his own decisions. He had a steady girlfriend, and if he did not continue in school he had to consider some kind of full-time employment to get on with his life, his future.

At this time Clara and Ben, not a minor anymore, could sell Max's house. The situation had been discussed with Pa Mintz, and Ben was to come into the store full-time and draw a salary. In order for this circumstance to come about, part of the money from the house went into getting more stock. The store had been doing well for many years. Ben had worked in the store since he was old enough to wield a duster and a broom. He had learned the business and, as he grew older, liked it more and decided that would be his life's work.

Pa Mintz bought a car. He didn't drive, but Ben did, taking Pa Mintz to the towns like Stillwater, Red Wing, and others, to get orders of shoes. They got along very well. Pa Mintz loved to go on the drives; they stopped and had lunch and talked. Many nights Ben drove the folks around, especially on warm evenings; then he could get the car to take his girlfriend out.

Pa Mintz's son-in-law came to help on Saturday nights and Sundays. People came from all over to buy shoes at the B. Mintz Shoe Store.

Ben married his girlfriend, Lena Kessel, a friend of Sarah's. Ben used the little money he had left to make a down payment on a house around the corner from the store. Ben and Lena had three sons: Michael, Bob, and Bill.

But as Clara's children grew up there were changes taking place in the world. The world was still healing the wounds of World War I, but the democratic powers that were victors in that war unknowingly were permitting a second, more terrible, war to come.

It began in 1922 when Italy, under Mussolini, became a totalitarian state and Mussolini a dictator. Totalitarianism developed in the countries defeated in World War I or countries unhappy with treaty arrangements or economically collapsed and socially demoralized. Germany was one of them.

In 1933 Adolf Hitler, known thereafter as the Führer, became chancellor of Germany, the start of a Germany he would call the

Third Reich. He put together the Berlin Axis, which included Japan, Italy, Spain, and Hungary. When the Nazis came to power they began a new reign of terror of anti-Semitism. It took them just a few years to sow the beginnings of what would become known as the Holocaust.

Jews were driven from offices in the government, army, and professions. They were isolated and restricted as to where they could live and where they could go. This was an important part of the German plan to destroy them. Across the Reich, bonfires were lighted with books of the intellectuals, dedicated to the extinction of Jewish influence on literature.

There were anti-Semitic attacks with physical abuse against Jews, all made legal by laws—as before during World War I.

The attacks began by individuals, then groups; then they would stop for a while. When the attacks were halted the Nazis waited for world reaction. If there had been an outcry against this abuse, the Nazis might have stopped it, but the rest of the world kept quiet, and the Nazis thought this a sign giving them the go-ahead to continue.

Then in 1938 came the madness and violence of *Kristalnacht* in Germany, where windows of shops and businesses were smashed and stores and synagogues and homes set on fire. Jews were beaten and killed. It was enough reason for thousands to emigrate late in 1938 and early 1939. Then it was too late—other countries hadn't made room for Jews who might have left Germany. Concentration camps were built across Europe.

The world and America began to hear about Hitler and his policies concerning Jews but thought the problem didn't concern them. It was far away. They were wrong!

In 1938, at a meeting concerning refugees (how to deal with Jews), world powers came to it without a program to accept Jews. The Nazis took this to mean the powers didn't want to take the Jews because they felt the same way Germans did.

Hitler began to swallow small countries—first was Austria. He then eyed Czechoslovakia, rich in national resources and industry. The Czechs thought they had powerful friends in Great Britain and the United States and France and the Soviet Union were prepared to support her.

Hitler constantly blustered and stormed at the Czechs and threatened Britain and France. He wanted the Sudetenland (the part of Czechoslovakia along the German border, where some 3 million Germans lived). Britain's prime minister, Neville Chamberlain, wanted the Czechs to surrender, thinking giving the country to Hitler would stop his policy of aggression and stop war. Betrayed by her friends, the little country of Czechoslovakia surrendered. Neville's policy came to be known as appeasement.

The Germans invaded Poland in 1939, then opened up an all-out war in which millions of Jews and others were murdered.

From 1939 to 1941, when the Soviet Union came in to take its share of Poland for helping Germany, millions of Jews came under German control and were put in ghettos. They left their homes and wealth. Everything was confiscated and they were forced to endure poverty, hunger, and slave labor and torture.

It was April 1940 when Germany invaded Denmark and Norway and then took the Low Countries of the Netherlands and Belgium. It was shortly after that France surrendered, in June. Germany was at the height of its power and planned to take Great Britain, but the Royal Air Force stopped her.

Hitler planned on taking the Soviet Union, too, and plans were made for mass murder and other ways to attack Jews again.

Special SS groups, known as *Einsatzgruppen*, were formed to carry out killing orders. They were shooting squads with special rank and traveled behind the German front lines, with first choice of transportation. They had the most important job in the military— the killing of Jews.

As the German army went on its blitzkrieg through the Soviet Union, Jews were trapped and caught. Killing squads right behind the front-line armies would round up the Jews from the villages and towns, take them away nearby, and shoot them. These Germans were directed to murder every last Jew. Brutality was the law.

These groups were very successful in killing Jews. Some kept daily counts of deaths of men, women, and children, and they ran to over a million and a half.

But the mad Nazis found this was not the best plan for exterminating Jews. They found several things wrong with it. The use of bullets was too "expensive" and too "slow." They had to find a cheaper way of killing these defenseless human beings—Jews!

They decided on the gas chambers and death camps, which led to the killing camps at Auschwitz, Treblinka, and others, which were in Polish territory controlled by the Nazis. They transplanted 3 million Jews across Europe, saying they were being relocated. They went to their deaths instead. This was a huge undertaking—time-tables to be met, all kinds of carts and wagons hired from the non-Jewish people—and crossing points had to be organized for this tremendous effort.

One by one Jewish communities were taken, registered, put in special areas in towns, taken to camps where they were held, then sent to Poland, where they were killed and cremated.

Thousands were involved—they could be seen standing at crossings watching, shaking their fists, shouting at the unfortunate Jews going to their deaths in cattle cars. Still when the war was over and these many were questioned, they straight-faced lied, saying they had not seen or heard anything.

In Poland, 90 percent of the Jews died. Poland and its people have to live with that record.

In a country like Denmark, the government and the people protested. The whole country insisted Jews were Danes—they couldn't be separated. And at great risk to themselves, the Danish non-Jews hid and protected 95 percent of Jews that were saved. Denmark and its people will stand forever as a shining example of humanity.

In Bulgaria the churches spoke out against what was happening to the Jews, and some churches in France did, too, but in Slovakia the churches supported the mass murders. How did they justify that with their religion?

The inhuman, barbaric Germans, at one point, felt they were using too much money to do their job of killing Jews. Using the gas Zyklon was too expensive. They saved more than half the money by using less Zyklon, which doubled the time it took for a poor Jew to die in the gas chamber.

Nazis' unspeakable brutality came through again when they decided to burn Jewish children alive in the camps so as not to waste money on gas. The gas chambers were so efficient, disguised as places to take showers, that at Auschwitz approximately thirty-four thousand people were exterminated every twenty-four hours!

The world also learned trains carrying troops were often stopped and held to give "priority" to trains carrying Jews to their deaths.

While all this was going on, the United States tried to stay out of the war, but on December 7, 1941, Japan attacked Pearl Harbor in a sneak attack, sinking so much of our naval power, with such a huge loss of life, that the country was horrified. America entered the war, and fought the Germans as well as the Japanese in the Pacific.

Tobie's husband joined the navy. Rosie's husband joined the Merchant Marine. Sarah's boyfriend, Joe Daniels, was in the air force, and they were married while he was in the service. Slovie's husband went to school at night, learning welding, hoping he could repair airplanes and war equipment. The government needed them. However, because of a physical disability, Sam was classified 4-F.

World War II was a long, cruel war for families all over the world and in our America. The country went into action buying War Bonds to support our war effort. Men who didn't have jobs now could find them in anything to do with the war effort. Women did everything, working in defense plants and taking care of homes and children with ration books.

It was a sad time for the country and the world. Americans stayed glued to the radio every evening to hear Walter Winchell begin his evening broadcasts seriously, "Good evening, Mr. and Mrs. America and all our ships at sea," and then in a somber voice relate all the bad setbacks the Allies had suffered that day.

It went that way for months. The Allies seemed to be losing the war—planes downed, armies pushed back, and convoys of ships with supplies sunk by German U-boats. The newscasts ended and people sat around looking terribly worried for families and our boys over there. They talked in hushed tones and went to bed hoping the news would be better tomorrow.

Hitler and his Axis friends had conquered most of Europe. The Battle of Britain caused the United States more worry. The Britons were bombarded all day and all night. Americans worried how much longer they could hold out—and tried to go about the business of everyday living.

The number of our dead grew—published daily in the paper. Everyone had different views of what should be done. What was being done was evidently wrong, according to them, but the country, no matter what its views, stood together, working together, sacrificing, hoping to end the terrible war.

The West Side sent many of its finest young men. Some families paid high prices! To walk into Chessed Shel Emes Cemetery and see the three tall monuments for the three Liebfeld brothers, casualties of the war, is an experience one doesn't forget, and there were many others.

The boys came home to a country devastated by the war with Japan and Europe, so many casualties, so many prisoners, so many missing in action, and, slowly trickling through, the world heard again of the atrocities perpetrated overseas.

The world had heard about the policy Germany was pursuing, a policy of extermination of Jews. At war's end, 6 million Jews had been eliminated by torture—burned in crematorium ovens, gassed—and the world had stood by and let it happen. The world learned the stories of the Holocaust were true, but the hate-mongers still dispute it.

The husbands of Clara's daughters came home and picked up the pieces of their lives and started over.

Sarah's Joe came home and worked for the government. Sarah became a bridal consultant and used her many creative talents for lovely weddings, bar and bat mitzvahs, and parties. They adopted a son, Richard, "Ricky."

Tobie's Jerry went to work for a jeweler, Mr. Kay, learned the business, then he and Tobie moved to California. They opened their own shops, Mr. B's, and did well working together. Tobie used her artistic talent in the store selling the beautiful pictures she made with dried flowers.

Rosie's husband, Clayton, started out in real estate and became very wealthy. Rosie was a wonderful wife who had struggled with him during the lean years, and they had three children. It saddened the whole family when Rosie and Clayton were divorced.

This was a source of great pain for Clara, having gone through it herself, now living it over again with her daughter. Slovie, having been a child old enough to remember the pain of divorce, suffered along with her sister and the children. There had always been a close sisterly bond between these two, and it just grew stronger during the years of hardship for Rosie. As life went on, Slovie and Rosie were always together, with a great respect and love for each other. Not only were they sisters, but best friends as well!

Sometimes it's hard to accept a crisis in life. Then when it is over, some of the hurt and anger may remain; the worst has been conquered, and life goes on to better things, and so it was with Rosie. She accepted the hand dealt her and met the challenge. She went to work and came out a stronger person, with a stronger faith. She raised her children, who made her proud, and made a new life for herself with many friends and was happy in a long marriage to a very nice man, Morrey Brown.

In 1948 Pa Mintz became ill with cancer and died. He was seventy-five years old, and he and Clara had been married for over twenty-three years. Like all marriages, it had its ups and downs, but Pa Mintz loved Clara and knew she had been a good, loving wife. His family still didn't accept her and took her to court to contest his will. Clara, Ben, and Al did get the store. Even though the early years were painful, Pa Mintz knew Clara's children had respected him as few children do.

In 1950 Albert went to the Korean War. When he came back, he married his childhood sweetheart, Rosie Manovitz. They had four children, Bryan, Douglas, Bradley, and Hannah.

Albert used his creative talents when he opened Bryan's Beauty Salon. He had other talents too, and for many years entertained in musicals for the Jewish community. His Tevye in *Fiddler on the Roof* always received standing ovations.

Clara finally got her house, where she had a flower garden she loved and on the Fourth of July, Flag Day, and Memorial Day was proud to fly the American flag!

When Ben's children were grown, his dream came to fulfillment. He entered classes in law at the University of Minnesota.

Slovie went to Europe and saw the many faraway places in her beloved books, then entered the College of Liberal Arts at the University of Minnesota.

For them and Clara—dreams came true.

When Clara was seventy-five she had her first heart attack. Slovie, Rosie, Albert and Sarah took turns caring for her. Then she had two more heart attacks and was almost blind before she went into Sholom Nursing Home. She was not left alone; her children visited her, and Slovie and Rosie cared for her constantly.

When Clara was eighty-five, her children, grandchildren, and great-grandchildren gave her a wonderful birthday party.

In 1984, two months before her ninetieth birthday, Clara died. Slovie had learned to cope with many things, but this, her mother's death, she couldn't deal with. She stayed with her in the room late into the night. Then Clara was taken away, as the Jewish burial rites had to be performed.

One of the hardest things Slovie ever had to do was make her mother's funeral arrangements. She went to pick out the casket and picked a plain oak one that had a Star of David on the top of it.

Slovie couldn't describe her feelings at that time. It seemed as though she were standing outside of herself, watching all this being done by someone else. She wondered out loud, worried how they were going to get her mother into the half-opened casket. She wasn't thinking logically. The man in charge put his hand on her shoulder and gently told her the whole top of the casket came off and they would be very careful with her mother. Slovie started to cry.

There was so much she hadn't thought about that had to be done. She wrote the obituary column. Now she understood the pain the people writing obituaries went through. She empathized with them, and her heart ached.

She went to the rabbi to tell him about her mother so he could give a nice sermon about her. Slovie was restless and tired, and walked around like a zombie but had to function. It was all up to her. Clara had taught Slovie her lessons well.

The chapel was filled. Clara's handsome grandsons were pall-bearers. She had loved them all. As the casket went out, Slovie realized a most important chapter of her life was ending. She would never see her mother again, and she could never speak to her or be with her again. It was difficult for Slovie to accept. One of life's forces had struck her a blow. She would have to recover and emerge again.

The family sat together in the limousine following the hearse, each one silent, with mixed thoughts and feelings.

Ben, sitting in front, turned and looked quite serious. "You know, Slovie, you were always a role model for us—for us to look up to. When we couldn't trouble Mom, we all knew we could come to you at any time, and you were there for us.

"You notice," he continued on, "we all did just that at one time or another, and you took the time to listen, and care and help."

Slovie looked at her family—they had all been through much growing up together. They were survivors!

"Thanks, Ben." She said it softly through a choking in her throat. She had never thought of it that way. She was the "oldest," and that made her caretaker!

After the funeral, everyone came back to the Apples' house to sit *shiva*. It's a time when mourners are at home to receive condolences and visits from relatives and friends. The *shiva* candle, symbolic of the soul, burned in the house of mourning for three days.

Slovie was glad when the *shiva* period was over. They had to try to pick up the pieces of their lives and go on. Her mother's death made Slovie come smack up against her own mortality. It left her with different feelings about the realities of life, the unimportance of so many things she had thought were important before.

To Slovie her mother would always be with her from the past, and now the present was important to her. She had never known her grandmother and always missed her. This made a great impact on her. So she wanted to be an especially caring grandmother to her grandchildren and gave them her love and biggest bear hugs, and they gave them back. It helped compensate in a little way for the feelings of loneliness she had when she was growing up.

When Clara looks down at her family, there are some things that make her sad. She must have wept with them when Ben died, the first broken link in the chain of siblings.

Then Tobie died and it was difficult to lose one of the three sisters. It was a time to let the good memories overshadow all others and so ease the pain.

There is great pride for Clara, too, for among her children, grandchildren, and great-grandchildren, there are those with degrees in medical sciences, law, art education, music, and social work, as well as authors and those in business. In America it could happen, and it did.

Clara is the only member of her family buried in a Jewish cemetery with a tombstone on her grave. It reads: "Clara, beloved wife, mother, grandmother, and great-grandmother." Every spring there are flowers growing in a planter Slovie installed on her grave.

Slovie misses her mother—her warmth and humor—and every so often gets an ache to touch her once more. Clara left her no heirlooms of value; she had none. She left something far more precious—the wonderful memories of them together through the years. Slovie would speak of her mother often and remember so many things—the stories she told of her father, Benjamin, and her mother, Slovie. The wonderful stories that were a beginning of their history!

A history is stories—stories of memories of yesterdays that give us a sense of who we are—and it's the influence of all the parts of our ancestors that shapes our todays. A blessed family's history goes on and on. It's a story that never ends and has its effects on all our tomorrows!

Epilogue

Our family history began with anti-Semitism. Anti-Semitism lived in the wars in Europe. It lived in America!

After World War II and the 6 million Jews annihilated in the Holocaust, where could the responsibility be put? Should it be on those who were there and did nothing to stop the Nazis? Should it be on those who were in power in Great Britain, America, and the other allied countries?

They could have helped, but other things were more important. This did not include Jews—6 million Jews!

Heads of governments and religious leaders of some churches give their sermons that incite anti-Semitism and deny—yes, *deny*—there ever was a Holocaust. To listen to them espouse their lies and hate is frightening.

"It wasn't going to happen again," but anti-Semitism lives. It is more widespread in America and all over the world than ever before. It will be as long as there are wars and governments in trouble and there is a need for scapegoats. They will use us—Jews!

We live with hope—and while we hope—there will be an end to the hate—we have to always be vigilant and speak out whenever we see or hear anything anti-Semitic. To be quiet is to commit the ultimate sin. Then part of the blame is with us Jews.

Stand up to the bigots—defend the Jew in you and other Jews! We must remember to tell the story of the Holocaust from generation to generation—not to forget.

God says to forgive. How do we forgive when we have to remember the Holocaust! We must remember, never forget!

Bibliography

Carran, Betty. *Enchantment of the World—Romania.* Chicago: Children's Press, 1988.

Dimont, Max I. *Jews, God, History.* Jewish Heritage Classics Series. New York: Viking, 1976.

Gilbert, Martin. *The Second World War.* New York: Henry Holt and Company, 1989.

Giurescu, Constantin C. *Transylvania—The History of Romania.* London: Garnstone, 1969.

Hale, Julian. *The Land and People of Romania.* Philadelphia: Lippincott, 1972.

Karp, Abraham. *Golden Door to America.* New York: Viking, 1976.

McLellan, Jill. *Romania in Pictures.* Visual Geography Series. New York: Sterling, 1970.

Pakula, Hannah. *The Last Romantic.* New York: Simon & Schuster, 1984.

Rittner, Carol, R.S.M., and Sondra Meyers. *The Courage to Care.* New York: University Press, 1986.

Shirer, William L. *Rise and Fall of the Third Reich.* New York: Simon & Schuster, 1960.

Speer, Albert. *Inside the Third Reich—Memoirs.* New York: Macmillan, 1970.